INFLUENCE OF ALICE 3: REDUCING THE HURDLES TO SUCCESS IN A CS1

PROGRAMMING COURSE

Tebring Daly, B. Ed., M.S.

Dissertation Prepared for the Degree of

DOCTOR OF PHILOSOPHY

UNIVERSITY OF NORTH TEXAS

May 2013

APPROVED:

Scott Warren, Committee Co-Chair
Cathleen Norris, Committee Co-Chair
Lin Lin, Committee Member
J. Michael Spector, Chair, Department of Learning
    Technologies
Herman L. Totten, Dean of the College of
    Information
Mark Wardell, Dean of the Toulouse Graduate
    School

ACKNOWLEDGEMENTS

I would like to express my deepest appreciation to my committee chair, Dr. Scott Warren, who has spent countless hours helping me to formulate and analyze this paper. I would also like to thank my dissertation committee, Dr. Cathleen Norris and Dr. Lin Lin, for their support and encouragement. Dr. Norris has been exceedingly helpful with guiding me through the doctoral program and Dr. Lin has always been willing to provide a helping hand. I have enjoyed my time at the University of North Texas and I would like to thank my fellow classmates for their reassurance and friendship. I want to give a special thanks to Debra Blackwell and Amy Trombley for helping me to analyze my qualitative data.

I would like to express my gratitude toward the National Science Foundation for their assistance to help fund this endeavor. My fellow National Science Foundation grant team members also deserve special thanks, especially, Dr. Wanda Dann and Anita Wright. They have been tremendously supportive throughout the duration of the grant and this dissertation.

My department dean and coworkers have been exceptionally accommodating to my obligations as a doctoral student. Thank you for being so understanding.

I am fortunate to have wonderful friends that helped me to stay focused and achieve my goals. Thank you for keeping me motivated.

I would like to give a heartfelt thanks to my family, especially my parents, Arthur and Eileen Wrigley. They have been extremely loving, patient, and supportive throughout this whole process. I would not have made it this far without them. Thank you for believing in me. I can't thank you enough. Finally, I would like to thank my amazing husband, Timothy Daly, for being there for me when I needed him most. He has endured many hours of dissertation "torture." I thank you with all my heart.

TABLE OF CONTENTS

LIST OF TABLES

LIST OF FIGURES

CHAPTER 1

INTRODUCTION

Many students struggle with learning how to write software (Bonar & Soloway, 1983;

Mow, 2008; Lahtinen, Ala-Mutka, Jarvinen, 2005; Robins, Roundtree, & Roundtree, 2003).

Students need to learn the syntax and semantics of a programming language as well how to

connect the two in order to solve a problem (Soloway, 1986). This process can be frustrating for

students. Successful programmers tend to be logical, analytical, and detail-oriented (Daly, 2010);

this affords them the ability to develop algorithms, synthesize problems, and troubleshoot errors.

In order to execute a program, you must adhere to the syntax of the language; any slight

deviation from the rules of the language (improper capitalization, misspelling, missing or wrong

number of braces, quotes, semicolons, brackets, and/or parenthesis) and the program will not run.

This can be overwhelming for students just learning how to program. Ultimately, they will need

to be problem solvers, to think abstractly, to be detail-oriented, and to be able to communicate

with peers in order for their code to tie into someone else's code, but this is too much to take on

at one time.

1.1   Statement of the Problem

Many students today are visual learners, yet programming is still taught in an abstract

environment focusing on computations (Fowler et al., 2000). Not only is the environment

abstract, but students are forced to be detail-oriented using a programming language that they are

not familiar with to debug syntax errors. They are also forced to deal with run-time and logic

errors. Students tend to have difficulty visualizing the programming concepts that are needed to

write the code. Since programming is such that one concept builds upon another, it is imperative

that they thoroughly understand each of the concepts before moving on. For example, you cannot

1

teach a student about parameters for methods if they do not understand the concept of a method or a variable.

Not only are traditional programming concepts hard to teach (Mow 2008), but many computer science classes add another complexity to the mix by teaching programming using the object-oriented paradigm (Schulte & Bennedsen, 2006). Paradigm and language choices in education are often dictated by the industry (Dingle & Zander, 2001). Java is the primary language choice being used to teach students introductory programming (Schulte & Bennedsen, 2006). Java forces students to learn the traditional concepts: variables, methods, loops, arrays, etc. as well as the object-oriented concepts: classes, objects, inheritance, polymorphism, etc. It is hard to teach students about objects, when they cannot visualize the objects.

1.2   Purpose of Study

The purpose of this study is to determine whether Alice 3 software [1] can increase student self-efficacy levels in various areas of programming, can raise student engagement, and can raise student scores on various achievement milestones (assignments, exercises, and exam scores). The comparison will be made between a traditional programming course (control group) teaching programming concepts using the Java programming language and a course using Alice 3 and Java to teach programming concepts (treatment group).

---

[1] Programming environment created by Carnegie Mellon University, http://www.alice.org

1.3 Research Questions

The research questions to be addressed by this study are as follows:

1. Are there significant achievement and self-efficacy differences between students learning object-oriented programming with Alice compared to those learning in a traditional environment? (data includes scores on midterm exam, final exam, course percentage, course grades including withdraws, and self-efficacy growth measurements for each programming concept)

2. Do demographics play a role with achievement and self-efficacy between the students using Alice and the students using the traditional environment? (data includes scores on midterm exam, final exam, course percentage, course grades including withdraws, and self-efficacy growth measurements for each programming concept)

3. Do demographic variables impact student opinions of the Alice environment? (data includes ratings of the usefulness, enjoyment, and intuitiveness of the environment, and an analysis of qualitative reactions)

1.4 Overview of Dissertation

Chapter 1 provides an introduction to the dissertation including the purpose, hypotheses, definitions of terms, and limitations of the study.

Chapter 2 identifies literature relating to visual programming environments and their effectiveness thus far; it compares and contrasts several different environments. It introduces the Alice 2/3 environments and research studies that have been conducted using these tools. Chapter 2 describes the pedagogy used for this study and provides literature that supports using a Likert scale to measure self-efficacy for achievement.

Chapter 3 provides an in-depth description of the design of the Alice 2 and Alice 3 environments.

Chapter 4 lists the research methods used for data collection and analysis. This chapter includes the research design, participant and setting background information, research conditions, and details about the instrumentation tool.

Chapter 5 presents overall demographic frequency counts, a Cronbach's alpha test for instrument reliability, a regression analysis to determine how much impact self-efficacy has on course success, and ANOVA tests to determine accuracy of hypotheses.

Chapter 6 reveals emergent themes from the qualitative data, depicts five case studies that portray each theme, and expresses how tutors feel about the software.

Chapter 7 brings the quantitative and qualitative chapter results together and adds points of discussion. It also offers recommendations for future studies and a final conclusion.

1.5   Definition of Terms

- Compiling – checking programming code for syntax errors

- CS0 course – pre-CS1 computer science programming course that is usually aimed at students that are non-computer science majors or need more exposure to problem solving before taking the CS1 course

- CS1 course – first level college computer science programming course

- CS2 course – second level college computer science programming course

- CS3 course – third level college computer science programming course

- Integrated development environment (IDE) – software that provides programmers with the tools required to write, compile, and execute their programs

- Java™ – an object-oriented programming language

- Logic errors - caused by mistakes that yield incorrect results, but do not defy the rules of the language

- Syntax – rules of a language

- Run-time errors - are caused by invalid data. Run-time errors do not affect the compilation of your program thus the program will compile and execute, but it may crash or hang after execution

- Software development kit (SDK) – programming language specific tools that are needed to write code

- Syntax error – is caused when the user writes code that violates the rules of the language. A syntax error can be caused by incorrect capitalization, spelling mistakes, etc. The compiler informs the user of a syntax error by displaying an error message.

1.6   Limitations of Study

I was the designer of the curriculum materials and instructor for the Fundamentals of Programming course. Although this helps to provide consistency, it also might raise questions about objectivity. Finlay (2002) believes that researcher bias can be overcome by conducting meta-analysis throughout the research process. The "moral integrity" of the researcher is a key component to validating the "quality of the scientific knowledge produced" (Kvale, 1996, pp. 241-242). In this study, the students received the same journal entry questions and were asked to write a response to the questions. The researcher hoped to eliminate bias by using written journal entries instead of conducting interviews.

A mixed methods approach was used to address validity concerns. The qualitative data was analyzed by two peer reviewers to establish inter-coder agreement and eliminate possible bias.

Some of the students had prior programming experience that will lead to smaller gains in self-efficacy levels. Although this course is intended for students with very little or no previous programming experience, sometimes experienced students take the course as a refresher, to learn a new programming language, or as an elective. The qualitative data may not be generalizable to a larger population since the population studied may only be true to the native local population. The treatment group completed extra exercises and assignments using Alice; this extra work may have influenced the results.

CHAPTER 2

REVIEW OF LITERATURE

Logo[2] was developed in the 1960s, making it one of the pioneers for teaching

programming through visualizations (Petre, 2007). The environment features an area for entering

commands and a visual area that positions turtles on the screen according to the textual

commands. The design of the environment follows the constructivist view of acquiring

knowledge, where students actively explore the environment and troubleshoot issues that arise as

they write the code (Petre, 2007). Although the Logo environment can be used to teach basic

functional programming, it is more geared toward teaching mathematical principals.

A variety of educational visualization tools have been developed to teach students how to

program. Scott Grissom developed a survey to measure faculty opinions on the effectiveness of

programming visualization tools; he distributed this survey during the ITiCSE[3] conference in

Helsinki, Finland in the year 2000 and received 91 responses. This survey was modified and

redistributed during the ITiCSE conference of 2002 with 95 responses. The modified survey

showed the following benefits of using visualization tools in the classroom: teachers found

teaching more pleasurable (90%), increased student participation (86%), students believe that the

class is more fun (83%), increased student motivation (76%), helped to provide a conceptual

foundation of algorithms (76%), utilized technology in a meaningful way (76%), improved

student success (72%), and improved comprehension (62%). Although, many of these responses

were subjective since they were based on faculty observations, informal student feedback, and

informal questionnaires, 52% found an increase in student success that was measurable. Ninety-

---

[2] Massachusetts Institute of Technology (MIT) supports the Logo Foundation, http://el.media.mit.edu/logo-foundation/index.html

[3] Annual Conference on Innovation and Technology in Computer Science Education

three percent of the people taking the survey agreed that "using visualizations can help learners learn computing concepts" (Naps et al., 2006, p. 10).

2.1   Types of Programming Tools

One group of computer science panelists at SIGCSE[4] separated these introductory programming tools into the following categories: narrative tools, visual programming tools, flow-model tools, specialized output realizations, and tiered language tools. Narrative tools introduce programming logic in a storyboard fashion. Visual programming tools provide an environment for manipulating code segments and for graphically visualizing programming concepts. Many of the visual programming tools also alleviate the burden of syntax errors by providing a drag and drop code editor. Flow-model tools are useful for developing and visualizing complex programming algorithms. Specialized output realizations utilize robotics to increase motivation. Tiered language tools provide the user with a flexible user interface that can be adjusted based on experience level (Powers et al., 2006; Daly, 2009).

This study is focused on Alice 3, which can be considered a visual programming tool, a tiered language tool, as well as a narrative tool. In addition to the Alice environment, the researcher chose to discuss other visual programming tools and the research behind the effectiveness of those tools.

---

[4] Association for Computing Machinery's Special Interest Group on Computer Science Education

2.2 Studies using Visual Programming Tools

2.2.1 App Inventor Environment

The App Inventor™[5] environment uses a drag and drop interface to build applications for the Android™[6] platform phone. Users design the graphical user interface, drag and drop puzzle pieces that fit together to represent their code, and then test their code on an emulator or an Android device. The emulator included with the environment mimics an Android device. This environment helps to teach about variables, conditionals, loops, procedures, logic, events, and lists. App Inventor elements can be incorporated into apps that are going to be programmed using the Java SDK, software development kit; this allows users to practice Java coding without learning the intricacies of the Android framework. Writing apps for mobile phones follows an event-driven programming paradigm (sensors, button clicks, etc. determine the flow of the program), which is different from what is usually covered in a traditional CS1 courses that focus on programmer defined sequence of instructions.

The environment is free of charge and can be used on a Windows® operating system[7], Apple Macintosh® operating system[8] (Mac), or Linux® operating system[9]. To gain access to the environment, users must register for a Gmail™[10] account. All of the App Inventor files are stored online under the user's Gmail account. You need to have access to the Internet to access the software and your files.

---

[5] Supported by MIT, http://appinventor.mit.edu

[6] Android, http://www.android.com

[7] Microsoft Corporation, http://www.microsoft.com

[8] Apple Macintosh Corporation, http://www.apple.com/osx

[9] Linux Foundation, http://www.linux.org

[10] Gmail, http://www.gmail.com

The App Inventor website provides a wide range of tutorials with varying levels of difficulty. There are numerous resources available for educators on the web: forums, blogs, syllabi, sample projects, and textbooks. App Inventor was originally created by Google®[11]; it was released to the public in 2010 and terminated a year later. MIT took over this project and rereleased it again in March 2012. There are many articles written on how App Inventor could be used to teach logic or programming concepts, but the researcher was unable to identify any studies conducted on the effectiveness of the environment to teach to programming concepts (App Inventor Website, 2012). Figure 2.1 shows the design area of the App Inventor environment.

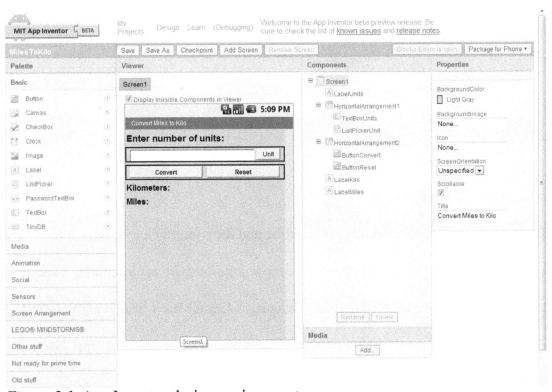

Figure 2.1. App Inventor design environment.

Figure 2.2 depicts the App Inventor coding drag and drop coding environment.

---

[11] Google, https://www.google.com/

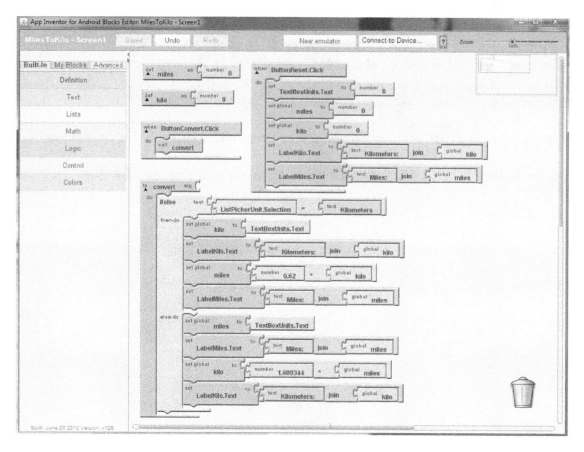

Figure 2.2. App Inventor coding environment.

2.2.2 GameMaker Studio Environment

GameMaker Studio™[12] environment uses a drag and drop interface to teach about objects, events, and variables. When students become more familiar with programming concepts, they can use the built-in GameMaker programming language. GameMaker Studio allows you to create executable files that can be embedded into a webpage and/or exported as an app. Users can publish their games to the YoYo Games©[13] website for others to play.

---

[12] GameMaker Studio, http://www.yoyogames.com/gamemaker/studio

[13] YoYo Games website, http://www.yoyogames.com/gamemaker/studio

YoYo Games, the creator of GameMaker Studio, provides downloadable tutorials listed on their site and a community forum for posting ideas. The tutorials include written instructions, examples of the game, and the resources needed to create the game. There are GameMaker textbooks that have been published for teaching students how to use this software. This software is available for the Mac and Windows operating systems and offered as a free limited-feature download or as a fully-feature paid download (YoYo Games Website, 2009).

Panitz, Sung, and Rosenberg (2010) measured the performance of 14 students in a CS0 course using a pre/post skills test and found that GameMaker improved comprehension of programming material. There was no comparison control group for this study and thus cannot be classified as statistically significant. The study also reported that five out of fourteen students felt that they would rather learn to code without the GameMaker environment. Figure 2.3 illustrates the GameMaker environment; this program has a tennis ball bounce off the side walls.

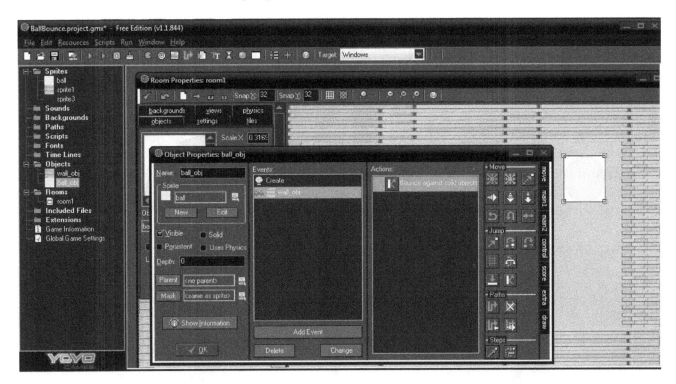

Figure 2.3. GameMaker environment.

2.2.3 Greenfoot Environment

The Greenfoot[14] environment provides students with a graphical representation of their code. They type Java code to animate two-dimensional objects and learn object-oriented concepts; they also have the option of making their program interactive. This environment helps to teach students about objects, statements, expressions, conditions, loops, variables, arrays, and events. The predefined objects that come with the software already include basic methods that students can use to get started, i.e., moving an object (Greenfoot Website, 2012).

The Greenfoot website provides basic videos and tutorials as an introduction to the environment. There are also discussion forums and textbooks that will help with teaching this software. Greenfoot can be downloaded free of charge and it runs on a Windows, Mac, or Linux operating system. This environment requires users to type the code.

Vilner, Zur, and Tavor (2011) integrated Greenfoot into a programming lesson on inheritance and found that many of the students enjoyed working with the environment and about half of the students felt that it helped them to understand the concept better. These results were based on the 325 out of 634 students that returned the course questionnaire.

Figure 2.4 and 2.5 show the Greenfoot environment in action. One of the creators of the Greenfoot environment, Michael Kolling, created a wombat scenario where wombats can move around the scene and collect leaves. This scenario is included in the Greenfoot installation folder; the user adds the wombats and leaves to create the scene and uses the predefined methods to have the wombats move, turn, and eat leaves.

---

[14] Part of the Computing Education Research Group at the School of Computing, University of Kent in Canterbury, UK, http://www.greenfoot.org

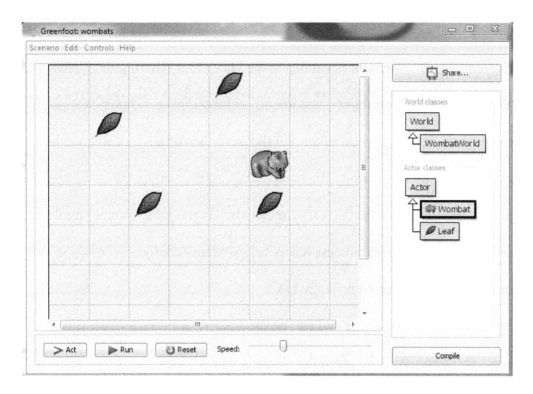

Figure 2.4. Greenfoot environment.

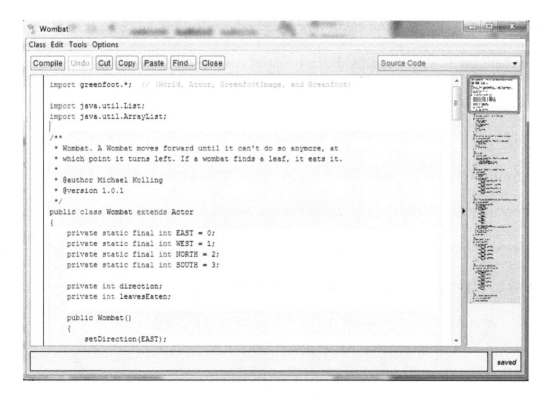

Figure 2.5. Greenfoot coding environment (code created by Michael Kolling).

14

2.2.4 Jeroo Environment

The Jeroo[15] programming environment is similar to the Greenfoot environment. This environment helps to teach students about objects, statements, expressions, conditions, loops, and variables. The Jeroo environment is structured around the metaphor of an Australian animal known as a jeroo which is similar to a kangaroo. The students program their jeroos using one of the following programming languages: Java, C++, C#, or Python. As the jeroo moves about the island, it must avoid any water or traps as it collects resources. Students configure the island and type the code to animate the jeroos (Jeroo Website, 2011).

Jeroo can be downloaded free of charge and can be used on the following platforms: Windows, Mac, or Linux. The Jeroo Website provides a variety of activities and assignments to accommodate varying levels of expertise (Jeroo Website, 2011; Daly, 2009). There are textbooks available for teaching programming using Jeroo.

Research shows that using the Jeroo environment can raise self-confidence levels and possibly raise comprehension of objects, methods, and control structures. Sanders and Dorn (2003) measured student programming confidence levels of 97 students before and after using the Jeroo environment; a paired t test showed that the confidence increase was statistically significant, but the p value was not reported (Daly, 2009). Within that same study, the three faculty members integrating Jeroo into their Java curriculum were solicited and overall they felt that students using Jeroo grasped the programming concepts of objects, methods, and control structures, more quickly. Figure 2.6 presents the Jeroo environment in Java mode; a jeroo named Tom was created and Tom turns and hops about the environment and picks up a flower.

---

[15] Jeroo website, http://home.cc.gatech.edu/dorn/jeroo

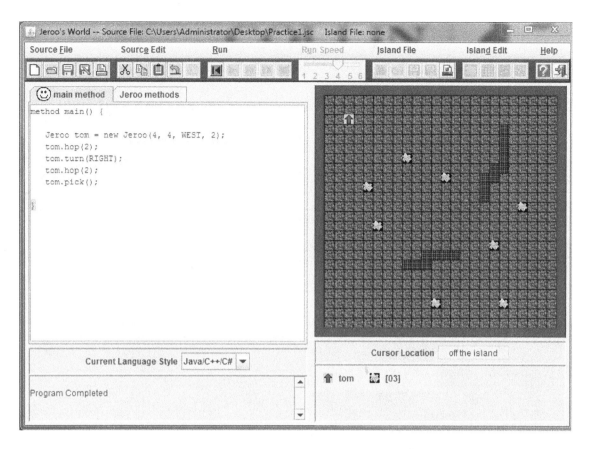

Figure 2.6. Jeroo environment.

2.2.5   Scratch Environment

Scratch[16] is a drag and drop narrative environment that allows the user to create programs by manipulating graphical blocks of code. This environment helps to teach students about objects, statements, expressions, conditions, loops, variables, threads, and events.

Scratch can be downloaded free of charge and can be used on a Windows or Mac computer. The Scratch Website provides tutorials and videos for getting started, a reference guide, forums, and a place for users to view and post finished Scratch projects (Scratch Website, 2012).

---

[16] Developed by MIT Media Lab, http://www.media.mit.edu

16

Scratch has been found to be an effective tool for introducing students to programming. Malan and Leitner (2007) surveyed 25 students and found that 76% believed that Scratch helped them to transition to Java, 16% thought that it had no impact, and 8% felt that Scratch had a negative impact. Sivilotti and Laugel (2008) questioned 30 eighth grade females using Scratch in a science and engineering summer camp and revealed that many students felt that Scratch was a valuable learning experience (mean 3.0 on a 4.0 scale) and fun to use (3.2 on a 4.0 scale) (Daly, 2009). Figure 2.7 depicts the Scratch environment; the cat was the basic default model and a dog was added to create an interactive animation.

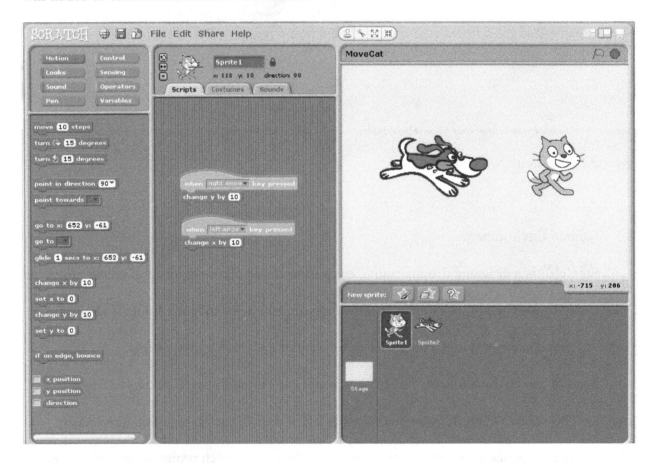

Figure 2.7. Stratch environment.

2.2.6   Alice Environment

Alice[17] combines features of the narrative, tiered language, and the visual programming tool. The environment uses three-dimensional objects to stress fundamental and object-oriented programming concepts, such as: objects, classes, inheritance, expressions, conditions, loops, variables, arrays, events, and recursion. Students formulate programs using drag and drop code segments rather than typing and worrying about the syntax of the language. Alice provides an environment where users can select a template, choose their objects, change the properties of their objects, program their objects, and manipulate the camera to create a story or an interactive game.

The software is written in Java and can be downloaded free of charge. It will run on the Windows, Mac, or Linux platform. There are two versions of Alice available for download, Alice 2 and Alice 3. Alice 2 is geared towards middle school and high school students; the environment is less complex and it does not give the user the option of exporting the Java code. Alice 2 is object-based; the models were created by CMU students. Alice 3 is object-oriented and can be used for more advanced students who want to expand upon the drag and drop interface and work with the Java code. Alice 3 has updated object models created by the Alice team at CMU and also includes some Electronic Arts Sims characters.

Although there have been quite a few textbooks published for Alice 2, Alice 3 was new and resources were not available for this version of the software at the time this study was written. The Alice website contains many Alice 2 resources for teachers, including: workshop information, newsletters, instructor syllabi, exams, projects, lecture notes, exercises, and much

_____

[17] Developed by Carnegie Mellon University (CMU), Alice, http://www.alice.org

18

more. Since Alice 3 materials were not available, the author chose to develop her own course materials.

Research shows that Alice 2 can raise performance rates, improve retention rates, and increase motivation towards programming (Cooper, Dan, & Pausch, 2003; Moskal, Lurie, & Cooper, 2004; Courte, Howard, & Bishop-Clark, 2006; Bishop-Clark, Courte, Evans, & Howard, 2007; Sykes, 2007; Johnsgard &McDonald, 2008; Daly, 2009; Mullins, Whitfield, & Conlon, 2009).

Cooper et al. (2003) measured the impact of students with no previous programming taking an Alice-based CS0 course before or concurrently with their CS1 course. The eleven students that took the CSO course with Alice 2 (treatment group) were compared to ten students that did not take the CS0 course (control group). It was discovered that the treatment group not only performed better than the control group, but they scored better than the students who had programming experience and did not take the CS0 course. Ninety-one percent of the students from the treatment group continued on to CS2, while only 10% of the students in the control group continued on to CS2. This study was done using a relatively small sample size.

Moskal et al. (2004) conducted a study to measure the effect of having at risk students take a CS0 course with Alice 2 before or during their CS1 course. The study was divided into three categories: treatment group which consisted of 25 students, Control Group 1 which consisted of 30 students, and Control Group 2 which consisted of 52 students. The treatment group was comprised of at risk students taking the CS0 Alice course, Control Group 1 had at risk students that did not take the CS0 Alice course, and Control Group 2 had students that were not at risk that did not take the CS0 Alice course. At risk students in this study, were classified as students with little or no previous programming experience and a weak math background. The study showed that the CS0 Alice courses had a higher retention rate (88% for at risk students) than the control groups (47% for at risk students and 75% for not at risk students). The at risk students using Alice 2 averaged a 2.98 grade point average (GPA), while the at risk students not using Alice 2 averaged a 1.18 GPA (Moskal, Lurie, & Cooper, 2004).

Sixty-four students out of approximately 100 students enrolled in an Introduction to Computers course participated in a study by Courte (2006). Alice 2 was used for three hours to introduce the students to programming. The students were given a pre-test survey before using Alice and a post-test survey after using Alice. Questions and responses from the survey were as follows: Generally I have felt secure about attempting computer programming (pre-test: 19%, post-test: 48%), I have a lot of self-confidence when it comes to programming (pre-test: 17%, post-test: 29%), I am no good at programming (pre-test: 26%, post-test: 16%), I like writing computer programs (pre-test: 10%, post-test: 27%), and programming is enjoyable and stimulating (pre-test: 11%, post-test: 37%) (Courte et al., 2006, p. 1).

Sykes (2007) did a comparison of CS1 courses not using Alice 2 (34 students) to CS1 courses using Alice 2 (72 students) at the same university. The Alice students and non-Alice students were asked a series of programming questions related to the course content. The Alice students scored statistically significantly higher, ($p < .044$). Although the Alice students scored higher, only 43% of the students believed that Alice was beneficial to them; Sykes believes that this could have been a result of the technical difficulties that students reported having with the environment. Fifty-one percent of the students found the Alice activities to be enjoyable and enrollment in the CS1 courses increased by 33% the year after the introduction of Alice into the curriculum; this could be coincidental or it could be a result of using Alice (Sykes, 2007).

Bishop-Clark et al. (2007) studied 154 students using Alice 2 for a 2.5 week period of time and found that it raised programming performance a statistically significant amount ($p <$ .001). Eighty-nine percent of the students "believed that they had learned the programming concepts and had gained a better appreciation of the complexity of programming" (Bishop et al., 2007, p. 205; Daly, 2009). In addition, when comparing the CS1 success rate of students who completed the CS0 course using Alice (37 students) with those who did not take CS0 (69 students), Johnsgard and McDonald (2008) discovered that the CS0 students had a higher success rate in CS1. The students that completed the CS0 course had an average success rate of 70% in CS1 compared to 46% for students without the CS0 course. Johnsgard and McDonald acknowledged that the effect may be attributed to the extra semester of programming.

Cliburn (2008) gathered the opinions of 84 students taking a CS1 course using Alice 2 as a seven week precursor to Java. Although 60% of the students felt that Alice helped them to learn Java and 67% recommended keeping Alice in the curriculum, there were mixed comments about the environment. Some students felt that Alice provided a visual representation and sparked creativity while others could not see the connection between Alice and Java. Cliburn mentioned that it would be helpful to repeat the study in the future for a CS1 course using Alice 3 and Java.

Mullins, Whitfield, and Conlon (2009) compared different types of courses using Alice 2. The first course, Introduction to Object-Oriented Programming, was taught with two different approaches: one using Alice (414 students) and the other using C++ (735 students). The Alice course sections had increased the female enrollment by 4%, increased success rates by 4%, decreased the withdrawal rate by 4%, and had a higher average GPA of 2.34 compared to 2.28. The second course, Objects and Data Abstraction, was taught using C++ (222 students) and

Alice transitioning to Java (91 students). The Alice to Java sections had a 5% increase in success

rate and an 11% decrease in withdrawal rate, but there was a decrease in GPA averages from

2.58 to 2.35 (Mullins, Whitfield, & Conlon, 2009).

In order to test the power of Alice 2 for teaching object-oriented programming concepts,

Linjawi and Al-Nuaim (2010) selected 21 student volunteers that completed an Introduction to

Programming course using C++ to attend an Alice lab (total of 14 hours over seven weeks). All

of the students were given a pre-test before taking the Introduction to Programming course, the

control group was given the post-test after the Introduction to Programming course, and the

treatment group was given the post-test after the Alice lab. The Alice group scored significantly

higher on the inheritance questions from the post-test (Al-Linjawi & Al-Nuaim, 2010).

Although a university received positive feedback from summer camp participants from

Grades 8-12 about using the Alice 2 environment, they did not have the same experience with

using Alice 2 as a two week precursor in a university CS1 course. The Alice courses (72

students) were compared to traditional courses (83 students) using pseudo-code. Both groups

covered the following concepts: variables, functions, methods, events, and loops. At the end of

the two weeks the students were given a problem and asked to draw the Alice code or write the

pseudo-code; the traditional students scored higher on this task ($p = .029$) and rated their

confidence levels higher than the Alice students (Garlick & Cankaya, 2010).

Only one study on Alice 3 was found. Dann et al. (2012) compared students in a CS1

course introducing Alice 2 for a two week period to two CS1 courses integrating Alice 3

throughout the course of the semester. The idea of mediated transfer was not used in the course

with Alice 2, since the software did not support transferring projects into Java code. There were

67 students in the control group (Alice 2 pre-cursor) and 50 students in the treatment group. The

students in both the control and treatment group were given the same exam and it was found that the treatment group performed better in the following areas: expression evaluation (13% increase), control structures (41% increase), arrays (18% increase), and class definitions (11% increase). Similar results were confirmed with a treatment group of 28 students the following fall semester (Dann et al., 2012).

While much research has been conducted on Alice 2, research on Alice 3 in particular has been limited. Although Alice 3 was created in 2009, it was not released from beta until 2012. This is what prompted the researcher to choose this study.

2.2.7   Summary of Visual Programming Tools

The Scratch, GameMaker Studio, and Alice 2 environments are very similar. They provide a drag and drop interface for creating animations and games. These environments focus on the logic behind programming rather than the syntax. In addition, they tend to be geared toward younger students.

App Inventor is similar to the Alice 3 environment. That is to say it allows users to go beyond the drag and drop code segments by transferring their program into Java code. This flexibility accommodates varying levels of expertise.

Greenfoot and Jeroo offer a similar type of programming environment. Instead of dragging and dropping code segments, the user must type the code. These environments provide a more natural transition into coding.

Many of the above tools have been shown to be effective for teaching programming to novices. GameMaker Studio has been shown to improve comprehension of programming material (Panitz, Sung, & Rosenberg, 2010). Greenfoot can be an exciting and useful way to teach inheritance concepts (Vilner, Zur, & Tavor, 2011). Research shows that Jeroo can raise self-confidence levels, as well as comprehension of objects, methods, and control structures (Sanders & Dorn, 2003 & 2004). Many of the students participating in the research felt that Scratch was an effective tool for transitioning to Java and an exciting and valuable learning experience (Malan & Leitner, 2007; Sivilotti & Laugel, 2008).

Several studies indicated that Alice 2 can help to raise performance rates, improve retention rates, and increase motivation towards programming (Cooper, Dan, & Pausch, 2003; Moskal, Lurie, & Cooper, 2004; Courte, Howard, & Bishop-Clark, 2006; Bishop-Clark, Courte, Evans, & Howard, 2007; Sykes, 2007; Johnsgard &McDonald, 2008; Daly, 2009; Mullins, Whitfield, & Conlon, 2009). One study found that Alice 2 caused an adverse effect on their courses (Garlick & Cankaya, 2010). Dann et al. (2012) showed that Alice 3 increased performance in the following areas: expressions, control structures, arrays, and class definitions.

2.3   Theory of Constructivism

Kanuka and Anderson (1999) stress that there are two dimensions of constructivism: how knowledge is constructed and whether a reality exists; these dimensions in turn create four constructivism positions: co-constructivism, situated-constructivism, cognitive constructivism, and radical constructivism. They define co-constructivism and situated-constructivism as socially constructed knowledge theories; whereas cognitive constructivism and radical constructivism are best described as individually constructed knowledge. Both co-constructivism and cognitive constructivism accept that there is an objective truth or an 'external reality' which one strives to represent.

Cognitive constructivism stresses that there is objective truth that we aspire to understand (ontology) and we reach this understanding by constructing knowledge based on our experiences (epistemology) (Kanuka & Anderson, 1999). This theory stems from the work of Jean Piaget (Hundhausen, 1999). In cognitive constructivism, knowledge is constructed by learners through the process of assimilation (Hundhausen, 1999). Assimilation is the process of organizing new experiences to fit within our existing schema of experiences (Siegler, 1998). If new experiences cannot be assimilated into our existing schema, one enters a state of disequilibrium and must reorganize the current schema to include the new experiences (Siegler 1998).

Cognitive constructivists would tend to introduce information as problem solving tools rather than as arbitrary facts (MacKinnon, 2002). Perkins (1991) asserts that teachers should present students with challenges to force them to construct better models; this construction causes change which results in knowledge. The cognitive constructivist theory focuses on the individual, but encourages social interaction to stimulate cognitive dissonance which in turn leads the individual to realize the inconsistencies of their understandings (Kanuka & Anderson, 1999).

Constructivism has already been successfully applied to science and mathematics education (Phye, 1997; Steffe, 1995). Ben-Ari (1998) and Hadjerrouit (1999) note that it can also be an effective way of teaching software engineering principles. Teaching students how to program computers provides them with new insights into their own thinking (Taylor, 1980, p. 245). The Alice 3 software gives students the opportunity to visualize abstract programming concepts by manipulating pieces of code in a drag and drop environment; they are able to create an object from a class, change the properties of the object, create methods for the object, and use other programming structures to maneuver the object. The objectivist epistemology may have worked for teaching procedural programming, but now that many software applications have shifted to object-oriented programming, which is a more abstract way of thinking, we need to reexamine our methods of teaching (Lanttazi and Henry, 1996).

2.4   Mediated Transfer of Concepts

Polya (1948) identified four basic steps in problem solving: understanding the problem, devising a plan, carrying out the plan, and looking back. Computer programming can be identified as having similar steps: determine input, process information, and output requirements; develop an algorithm and write pseudo code; translate pseudo code into the proper syntax rules of the language; finally, test and debug the program. It is important to teach students that programming is problem solving and that they need to work through each of the steps in an iterative fashion to arrive at a solution.

Alice 3 was integrated into the Java curriculum at the college under study for the treatment group with the hopes that the concepts learned in the Alice environment would transfer into the Java environment. This choice was in keeping with the findings of Dan et al. (2012) who found that using a "mediating transfer" approach from Alice to Java, helped to raise student achievement; the treatment group averaged at least one letter grade higher than the control group that did not use Alice. Programs can be written using the drag and drop interface in Alice 3 and transferred into Java code using the Netbeans[18] IDE. You can start a program in Alice 3, transfer the program into Netbeans, and finish it by writing only Java code.

---

[18] Supported by Oracle, http://netbeans.org

26

2.5   Measuring Self-Efficacy

This study has the students rate their self-efficacy level in understanding and applying various programming concepts. This measure of self-efficacy can aid in determining whether the Alice 3 environment is useful for helping students to gain confidence in a particular area.

In his social cognitive theory, Bandura (1993) proposed that self-efficacy plays a role in all aspects of life. He proclaimed that self-efficacy impacts our motivation, interest, and achievement towards specific tasks (1996). Students that are motivated are more involved in their learning and are therefore more likely to finish a course (Militiadou and Savenye, 2003). Students in that study were asked to rate their self-efficacy with each programming concept by using a Likert scale. The Likert scale was found to be an effective measure of self-efficacy for academic performance based on its reliability and validity (Mauer & Andrews, 2000; Maurer & Pierce, 1998).

CHAPTER 3

SOFTWARE DESIGN

3.1   Alice 2 Features

The user should first plan the animation/game that they want to create before setting up

the scene or assembling the code in the Alice environment. This can be done via basic story

boarding. The animations or games are referred to as worlds in Alice. When the user wants to

create a new world they must first select the template. The template is the basic background for

the scene, i.e. grass, snow, etc. Figure 3.1 shows the template choices.

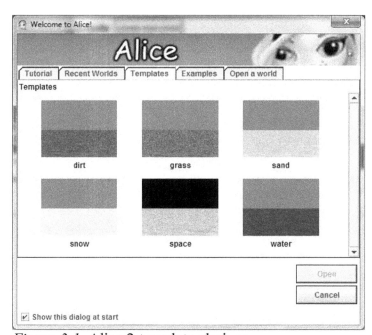

Figure 3.1. Alice 2 template choices.

After selecting a template, the user must then pick the objects that they would like to

incorporate into their world. The objects are broken down into categories based on type; these

categories are separated into folders. The categories are organized alphabetically. There are a

variety of objects to choose from; the object models were created by students at CMU, Carnegie

Mellon University. The blueprints for the models are known as classes, which is the proper programming terminology. When you choose to add an object from a blueprint, it will ask you if you want to create an instance of the class; this terminology helps to prepare students for terms that they will use when writing code. Figure 3.2 displays the galley choices.

Figure 3.2. Alice 2 object gallery.

The scene editor view allows for manipulation of objects; they can be resized, rotated, moved, copied, and/or deleted once they are added to the world. The user can manipulate the camera angle to create multiple scenes or focus on particular objects. Once the user is done setting up the scene, they can switch to the code editor view; this is shown in Figure 3.3.

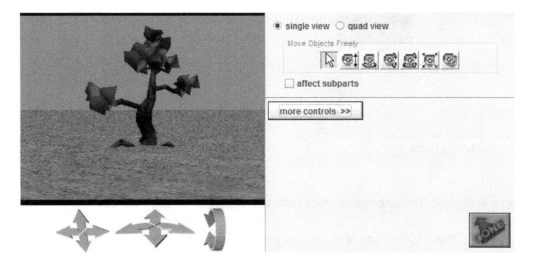

Figure 3.3. Alice 2 scene editor.

The code editor has an object tree which lists all of the objects in the world; a details pane which includes a property, method, and function tab; an event pane which is used for making the program interactive; and a code editor which is used for programming objects. Figure 3.4 displays the code for having a bunny hop forward during animation. This program uses basic programming constructs.

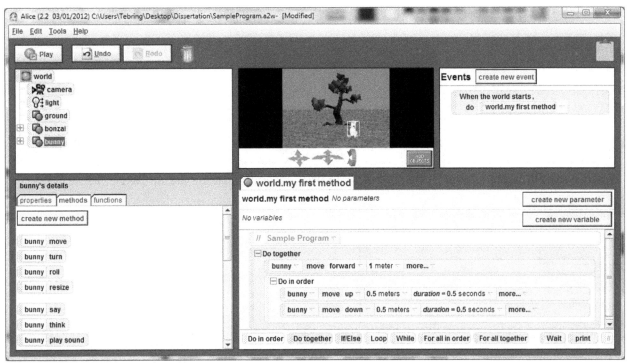

Figure 3.4. Alice 2 code editor.

The properties tab allows the user to change the properties of the objects in the world. The object must be selected before clicking on the properties tab. Figure 3.5 shows the property tab.

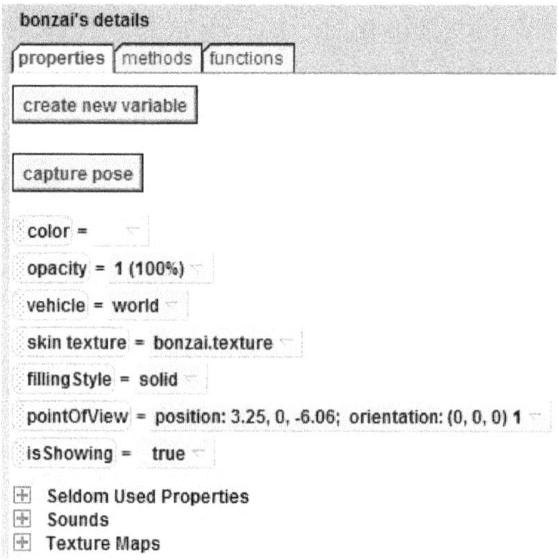

bonzai's details

properties | methods | functions

create new variable

capture pose

color =
opacity = 1 (100%)
vehicle = world
skin texture = bonzai.texture
fillingStyle = solid
pointOfView = position: 3.25, 0, -6.06; orientation: (0, 0, 0) 1
isShowing = true

⊞ Seldom Used Properties
⊞ Sounds
⊞ Texture Maps

Figure 3.5. Alice 2 property tab.

Methods supply the actions for the objects. The users can choose to use an Alice pre-defined method or create one of their own. The pre-defined methods are shown in Figure 3.6.

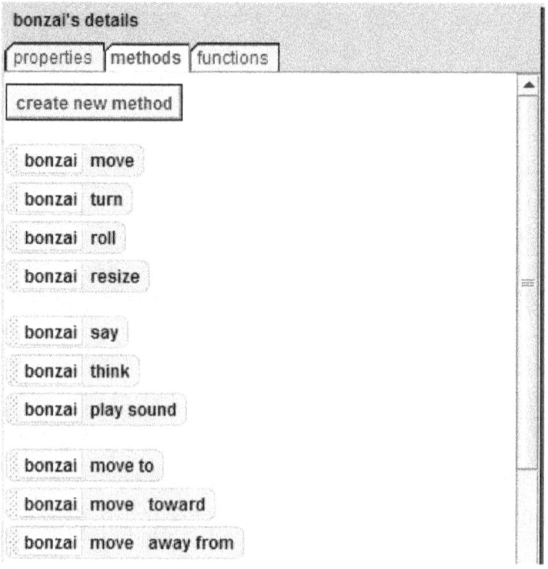

bonzai's details

properties | methods | functions

create new method

bonzai move
bonzai turn
bonzai roll
bonzai resize

bonzai say
bonzai think
bonzai play sound

bonzai move to
bonzai move toward
bonzai move away from

Figure 3.6. Alice 2 method tab.

Functions allow the user to ask questions about the environment. For example, if you wanted to calculate the distance from one object to another object, this would be a function. Alice includes pre-defined functions, but also allows the users to create functions of their own. Figure 3.7 lists the pre-defined functions.

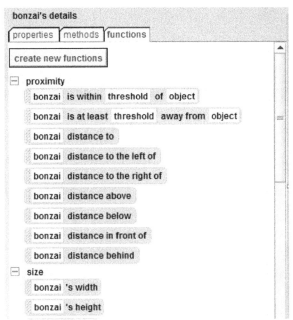

Figure 3.7. Alice 2 function tab.

Properties, methods, and functions, are not the only items that the user can select. The user can choose from the following commands to create more interesting programs and to practice with different programming constructs. Figure 3.8 lists the programming construct choices.

Figure 3.8. Alice 2 other commands

Alice 2 allows users to add objects to their world, to manipulate those objects, and to create or use pre-defined Alice methods or functions to program the objects. Conditionals, control structures, threading, and events can be used to enrich programs. Users can modify object properties and add documentation to enhance their programs.

3.2   Alice 3 Features

Alice 3 provides more functionality than Alice 2; it reveals the Java code behind the drag and drop environment. The structure of Alice 3 is designed around object-oriented principles: methods are created at the object level in Alice 2 and methods are created at the class level in Alice 3. The templates have been redesigned so that there are more template options. Figure 3.9 lists the template options.

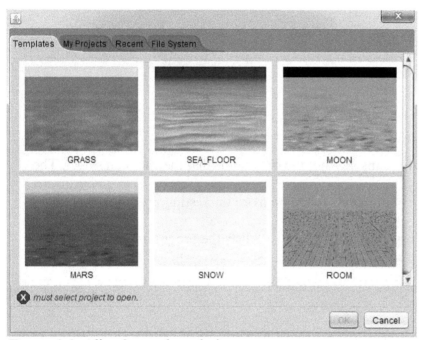

Figure 3.9. Alice 3 template choice.

The models are separated into folders based on their skeletal makeup. This type classification gives the objects a hierarchical structure that enforces inheritance rules of programming. Methods can be created for a higher level class such as biped and used for any biped class or can be written for a specific class such as alien which is a biped. The organization of classes and model can be seen in Figure 3.10.

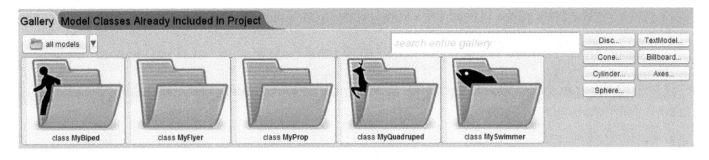

Figure 3.10. Alice 3 object gallery.

The scene editor is similar to Alice 2; it allows for manipulation of objects (resizing, rotating, moving, copying, and deleting), as well as object properties such as color, opacity, position, etc. It also includes markers for easily positioning objects on top of other objects, alongside other objects, etc. Figure 3.11 displays the scene editor.

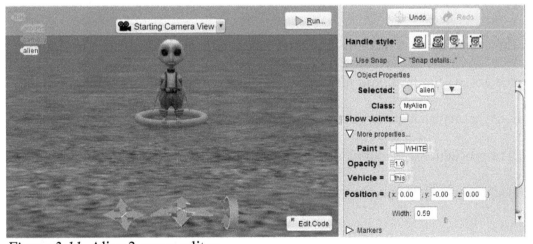

Figure 3.11. Alice 3 scene editor.

The code editor is used for adding procedures, functions, and/or adjusting properties during the animation. The default method for writing code is called "myFirstMethod." Figure 3.12 illustrates the code for having an alien say hello, look around, and question his location.

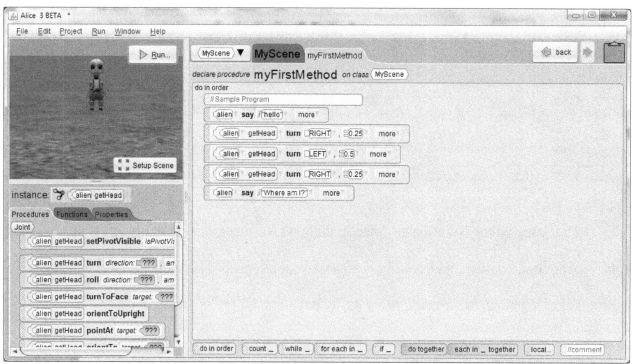

Figure 3.12. Alice 3 code editor.

The Alice environment splits methods into three categories: procedure, function, and property. The procedures are the Java void methods that do not return a value, the functions are the non-void methods that return a value, and the properties are the setter and getter methods for object properties. The procedures tab includes pre-defined and user-created procedural methods for the selected object (instance); this is shown in Figure 3.13.

Figure 3.13. Alice 3 method tab.

The functions tab provides a list of pre-defined and user-created functions for the object. Functions return data that can be useful for determining distance, selecting a body part, or deciding if an action should be taken. Figure 3.14 lists some of the pre-defined Alice functions.

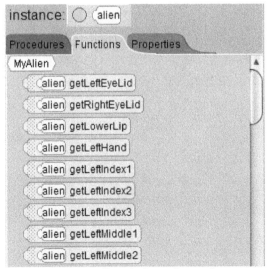

Figure 3.14. Alice 3 function tab.

The properties tab allows users to set and retrieve object properties. Changing the properties of an object before running the animation is handled during scene setup. A few of the property choices are shown in Figure 3.15.

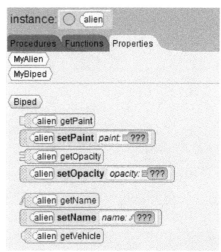

Figure 3.15. Alice 3 property tab.

The user can define and edit procedures, functions, and properties by selecting the class that they want to modify. Figure 3.16 shows the "MyScene" class options. Every project has a "MyScene" class that contains "myFirstMethod" which is run automatically.

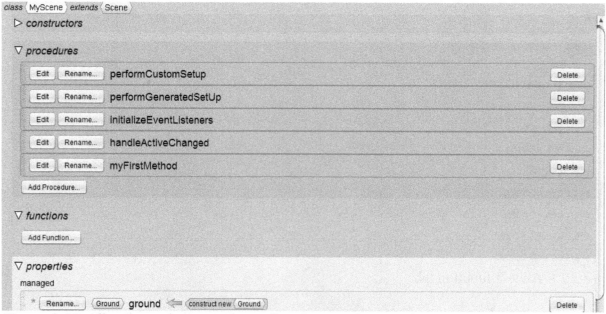

Figure 3.16. Alice 3 creating procedures, functions, and properties.

Alice 3 provides similar command blocks to Alice 2. These programming constructs are the basis of many programming languages. Figure 3.17 lists the command blocks.

Figure 3.17. Alice 3 other commands.

Alice 3 has many of the same features as Alice 2, but is geared toward more advanced students that are in the process of transitioning to coding (Alice Website, 2013). The structure of Alice 3 stresses object-oriented concepts and provides the capability of transferring an Alice project into an IDE to edit the Java code. Alice 3 was not written to replace Alice 2, but to serve as a tool to meet different audiences (Alice Website, 2013).

CHAPTER 4

RESEARCH METHODOLOGY

4.1   Hypotheses

This study examined Alice 3, a three-dimesional programming environment designed to visually teach users programming concepts. It included a combination of quantitative and qualitative methods. Qualitative methods were used to provide more depth into the user's reactions to the environment. Having both a quantitative and qualitative measurements helped to strengthen the results of this study.

The directional hypothesis of the first question is: The treatment group will have a statistically significant higher rate of achievement and self-efficacy than the control group.

The directional hypothesis of the second questions is: Females, students with no prior programming experience, and online students in the treatment group will have a statistically significant higher level of success and self-efficacy than those in the control group. It is predicted that there will be no statistically significant difference between the treatment and control groups with the following demographics: age, ethnicity, student status, number of credit hours earned, major, and semester.

The directional hypothesis of the third question is: Females, students with no prior programming experience, and online students will find the Alice environment statistically significantly more engaging, intuitive, and useful. It is predicted that there will be no statistically significant difference between the treatment and control groups with the following demographics: age, ethnicity, student status, number of credit hours earned, major, and semester.

4.2   Research Design

This study used a quasi-experimental comparison design to measure self-efficacy and achievement levels. Students registered for the Fundamentals of Programming course without knowing whether they would be in the treatment or control group. This course did not require any prerequisites to enroll.

The type of instruction is the independent variable and the self-efficacy and achievement levels is the dependent variables for this study. The author developed the instructional materials with a colleague from another community college. Students from both groups were given the same midterm and final exams. Those in the treatment group received Alice reading material, exercises, and assignments throughout the course as well as Java reading material, exercises, and assignments. The control group received only the Java reading material, exercises, and assignments. The Java material, exercises, and assignments were identical for both groups.

4.3   Setting

This study took place at a community college located in the south central region of the United States. The study was conducted at two different campuses. These two campuses are comparable in size and demographics. Both of these campuses are located within the metropolitan area of a major city. Please refer to Figure 4.1 and Figure 4.2 for the layout of each of the classrooms.

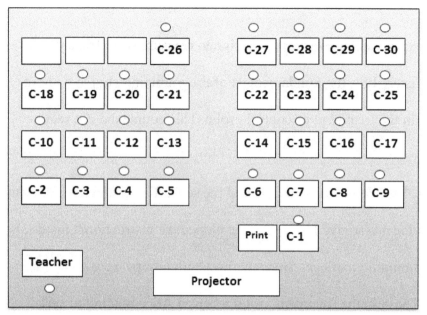

Figure 4.1. Classroom Layout 1.

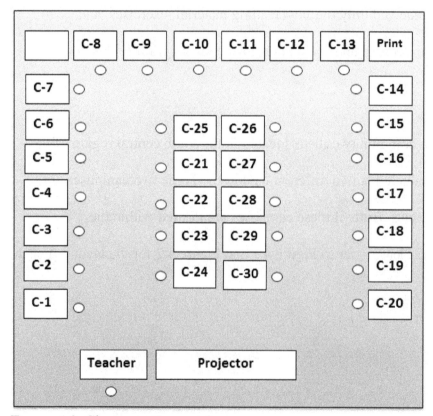

Figure 4.2. Classroom Layout 2.

4.4   Participants

4.4.1   Spring 2012

The participants consisted of community college students from four separate Fundamentals of Programming courses. Two of the courses were face-to-face courses scheduled in the afternoon and two were online. Since face-to-face and online courses can recruit different types of students, it was essential to break these courses down into treatment and control groups based on type. One campus was chosen to be the control group (Classroom Layout 1) for the face-to-face classes and the other was chosen to be the treatment group (Classroom Layout 2).

4.4.2   Fall 2012

The sessions were held constant for the fall 2012 semester; the face-to-face sessions were scheduled at the same time of day and the researcher used the same face-to-face and online session for the treatment and control groups.

4.4.3   Spring 2012 and Fall 2012 Evening Face-to-Face Courses

Since the campus location and classroom layout could create confounding variables for this study, treatment and control groups at the same campus, with same classroom layout, at the same time of day were compared. It should be noted that the comparable classes were taught in different semesters.

Data were collected from an evening face-to-face (treatment group) session during the spring 2012 semester, but were removed from the study due to a change in class structure and a low return on journal entries. There is reason to believe that this change in class structure could have led to the high withdrawal rate and the high number of non-successful students in this section. Since the online courses for the spring semester were full, students were given

42

permission to register for this face-to-face session and take it as an online class. The course was adjusted to accommodate students who wanted to participate online and those who wanted to take it face-to-face. All students were given the option to do the work online or to attend class. The students were required to submit all exercises as proof of participation. This classroom setup seemed to affect the student productivity level. Students that would not normally take an online class started taking this class online and failed to keep up with the pace of the course. Only one section of the evening face-to-face course was offered in the fall 2012.

4.5   Conditions

4.5.1   Both Groups

The author/researcher of this study worked with another colleague to design the materials for the courses and taught both groups of students. The chapter objectives are listed in Appendix D. The office hours were held at both campuses to ensure that the students had equal support. Tutoring was also made available to the students during the day and night at both campuses. Tutors were former students who did well in the course. There were five different tutors, three males and two females.

All of the notes, exercises, assignments, and exams for the courses were posted on Blackboard Learn™[19], a learning management system. Each face-to-face class session was recorded using Blackboard Wimba Classroom™[20], a collaboration tool used to capture the screen and audio. The videos were created to give online students another method of instruction besides reading the text and working through the exercises on their own, to give face-to-face students an

---

[19] Blackboard, Inc., http://www.blackboard.com

[20] Blackboard, Inc.., http://www.wimba.com/solutions/higher-education/wimba_classroom_for_higher_education

opportunity to replay explanations and hands-on coding practice, and to allow face-to-face students who missed class the ability to see what they missed. All of the videos were posted in Blackboard Learn.

The students were required to fill out seven journal entries throughout the course; these journals contributed to 10% of their overall grade. The journal entries measured self-efficacy, time management, knowledge, challenges, and reactions to the Alice software. The students received credit for the journal entries based on completion, not content.

All students were required to turn in the hands-on class exercises as proof that they worked through the exercises in the chapters; this accounted for another 10% of their grade. The hands-on exercises were created to help the students practice concepts learned in the chapters. The students were instructed to work through the exercises before working on the assignments. Assignments were used to reinforce concepts that were covered in the chapter material and hands-on exercises; the assignments were scored based upon rubrics and constituted 40% of their overall grade.

The midterm and final exams consisted of Java questions to test whether students were grasping the concepts. The students were allowed to use their notes, exercises, and assignments while taking the exams. The purpose of this course was not memorization, but to train them to use the resources that they had to solve problems. The exam scores combined made up 40% of their final grade. The Java assignments and exams were the same for both groups of students. Both groups of students used the Netbeans IDE for writing the Java code.

Throughout the course, the instructor presented the students with challenges while coding and probed the students for various solutions to the challenge; this helped to show students that there are multiple ways to solve a problem. Students were encouraged to communicate with one another via the discussion board in Blackboard. The students introduced themselves and actively carried out discussions. The students were given extra credit for participating in discussion board entries. Some of the discussion topics were: uses for Java coding, classes and method use, programming jobs, and programming and scripting language examples. The discussion board was also used to post student projects.

4.5.2 Treatment Group

The treatment group completed extra exercises and assignments using the Alice environment. They worked through exercises demonstrating the use of programming terminology by creating animations in Alice. The reason for using Alice in combination with Java was to use mediated transfer to teach the programming concepts. Please see the literature review for more information on mediated transfer. The journal entries also included students' attitudes toward the Alice environment.

4.5.3 Control Group

Since the author/researcher helped design the curricular materials and was the instructor for both groups, it helped to ensure that the comparison group did not receive any extra treatment that could hinder the results of the study.

4.6 Data Collection

The author/researcher of this dissertation was involved with an Advance Technological Education National Science Foundation grant entitled *Transition: Alice 2 to Alice 3 in Community Colleges*. The purpose of this grant was to integrate the Alice 3 software into basic programming courses and to train local college faculty members how to integrate Alice 3 into their curriculum. Three community colleges participated in this grant initiative. The researcher worked with one of the community college faculty members to develop curricular and training materials for teaching programming concepts using the Alice 3 software.

As part of this grant, the researcher required students in the Fundamentals of Programming courses to fill out seven journal entries throughout the course. The journals consisted of both quantitative as well as qualitative questions. The purpose of the entries were to gauge student reactions to the Alice software, their confidence with understanding and applying course concepts, their ability to manage their time, their knowledge, and their opinions on challenging class activities. All seven journal entries required the students to identify themselves and their course section number; this information was used to give the students credit for their entries, to match journal entries with grade information, and to make adjustments to the course based upon their answers. Some data were missing due to students declining to participate in the study or students withdrawing from the course.

4.7   Instrumentation

The first journal entry consisted of quantitative questions to collect demographic information, identify and measure prior programming experiences, gain insight as to the reasoning behind why students enrolled in the course, and measure self-efficacy for each programming concept. The following programming concepts were being measured: variables, objects, classes, procedural methods, functional methods, parameters, conditionals, loops, and arrays. Journals two through six contained Likert-scale quantitative questions to gauge student confidence levels with understanding basic programming concepts and with applying those concepts to solve a problem, to measure reactions to the Alice environment (enjoyment, ease of use, and usefulness), and to evaluate the use of resources.

Qualitative questions in Journals 2 through 6 were created to determine perceptions of the Alice environment. The last journal entry had students rate the following: their confidence in understanding each of the programming areas (high to low), the degree to which they felt that Alice contributed to their understanding of each of the concepts (high to low), and the engagement and ease of use of the Alice software (strongly disagree to strongly agree).

The control group was not given any questions regarding Alice. They were never exposed to the Alice environment and were unaware that a treatment group using Alice existed. The journal questions are located in the Appendix C.

CHAPTER 5

QUANTITAVE RESULTS

The data were collected as part of a federal grant and the archived data was used for analysis. The analysis starts with participant demographic information, then reliability testing of the instrument, testing of hypotheses, listing of case studies, and tutor reactions to Alice.

Data were analyzed using Statistical Package for the Social Sciences (SPSS®[21]) version 21. Only the students that completed journal one and agreed to the Instructional Review Board (IRB) were included in the survey. The IRB form is located in Appendix B. There were a total of 258 participants: 130 in the treatment group and 128 in the control group.

5.1   Participant Demographics

The participants registered for their course without knowing if they would be using Alice. The face-to-face classes at the participating institution are limited to 30 students and the online sections are limited to 25 students. Although all of the class sections started out full on the first day of class, some students dropped the course before the census date and some students declined to sign the Instructional Review Board (IRB) paperwork and therefore could not be admitted into the study. Table 5.1 presents the participant classroom distribution.

---

[21] IBM software, http://www-01.ibm.com/software/analytics/spss

Table 5.1

Treatment Group and Control Group Counts

Treatment Group			Control Group		
Semester	Type	Count	Semester	Type	Count
Spring 2012	Face-to-face afternoon	28	Spring 2012	Face-to-face afternoon	29
Spring 2012	Online	23	Spring 2012	Online	22
Fall 2012	Face-to-face afternoon	29	Fall 2012	Face-to-face afternoon	29
Fall 2012	Online	24	Fall 2012	Online	19
Fall 2012	Face-to-face evening	26	Spring 2012	Face-to-face evening	29
Total		130			128

5.1.1   Gender

Of 258 participants, 76% of the participants were male and 24% were female. This is not unusual; there have been many articles written about the lack of females majoring in computer science (De Palma, 2001; Stross 2008; Ashcraft & Blithe, 2009). Although 57% of women earned a bachelor's degree in 2008, only 18%of those were computer and information science degrees; this is down 37% from 1985 (Ashcraft & Blithe, 2009). Table 5.2 presents the participant gender frequencies.

Table 5.2

Gender Percentages

Gender	Frequency	Percentage
Male	195	75.6%
Female	63	24.4%

5.1.2 Ethnicity

The majority of the participants were Caucasian (62.8%). Asian (16.7%), Hispanic (9.3%), and African American (7.8%) made up the remaining majority of the participants. Table 5.3 shows participant ethnicities.

Table 5.3

Ethnicity Percentages

Ethnicity	Frequency	Percentage
Caucasian	162	62.8%
Asian	43	16.7%
Hispanic	24	9.3%
African American	20	7.8%
Multiracial	5	1.9%
American Indian	3	1.2%
Other	1	0.4%

5.1.3 Age

Of 258 participants, 59.3% were under 25 years old and 75.2% were under 30. Table 5.4 presents the distribution of participant ages in terms of range and frequency.

Table 5.4

Age Percentages

Age Groups	Frequency	Percentage
18-21	93	36%
22-29	101	39.1%
30-39	40	15.5%
40 and over	24	9.3%

5.1.4   Status (full-time or part-time)

The majority of students were attending college full-time (67.1%). Table 5.5 provides a break-down of the status frequencies.

Table 5.5

Status Percentages

Status	Frequency	Percentage
Full-time	173	67.1%
Part-time	85	32.9%

5.1.5   Number of Credits Earned

The amount of credits earned at of the beginning of the study varied across the group and are presented in Table 5.6.

Table 5.6

Credit Hour Completion Percentages

Credits Earned	Frequency	Percentage
Less than 15	82	31.8%
Between 15-30	47	18.2%
Between 31-60	81	31.4%
More than 60	48	18.6%

5.1.6   Class Type (Afternoon, Evening, Online)

There were a higher percentage of students in the afternoon sections. The online sessions have a lower class maximum and there were fewer sections of the evening classes offered. The face-to-face classes had a maximum of 30 students per class and the online classes had a maximum of 25 per class. The percentages of students in each class type are shown in Table 5.7.

Table 5.7

Class Type Percentages

Time of Day	Frequency	Percentage
Afternoon	115	44.6%
Evening	55	21.3%
Online	88	34.1%

5.1.7   Prior Programming Experience

More than half of the participants (54.2%) have had prior programming experience, not including HTML experience. Table 5.8 indicates the range of programming experiences from none to more than two programming languages currently known.

Table 5.8

Programming Experience Percentages

Experience	Frequency	Percentage
No Experience	92	35.7%
HTML Experience	26	10.1%
Scripting Experience	11	4.3%
One Programming Language	75	29.1%
Two Programming Languages	20	7.8%
More than 2 Programming Languages	34	13.2%

Participants were grouped into two categories based on their experience level. The students with no programming experience or only HTML experience were categorized as having "no experience." The students with scripting experience and/or experience with at least one programming language were counted as the "experience" group and accounted for 54.3%. Table 5.9 categories the students into two groups: experience or no experience.

Table 5.9

Grouped Programming Experience Percentages

Experience	Frequency	Percentage
No Experience	118	45.7%
Experience	140	54.3%

5.1.8 Major

Computer science (27.9%) and engineering (22.1%) were common majors for students enrolled in the Fundamentals of Programming course. The percentages of students based on choice of major are presented in Table 5.10.

Table 5.10

Major Percentages

Major	Frequency	Percentage
Computer Science	72	27.9%
Engineering	57	22.1%
Computer Information Systems	36	14%
Web Programming	22	8.5%
Gaming	12	4.7%
Science	11	4.3%
Business	7	2.7%
Mathematics	6	2.3%
Undeclared	23	8.9%
Other	12	4.7%

For data analysis, the participants were grouped into three categories: computer science majors, mathematics and engineering, and all other majors. Fifty-five percent of the sample consisted of computer science majors as seen in Table 5.11.

Table 5.11

Grouped Major Percentages

Major	Frequency	Percentage
Computer Science	142	55%
Math and Engineering	63	24.4%
Other	53	20.5%

5.1.9   Semester

The spring 2012 and fall 2012 semesters were almost equivalent. The percentages are shown in Table 5.12.

Table 5.12

Semester Percentages

Experience	Frequency	Percentage
Spring 2012	131	50.8%
Fall 2012	127	49.2%

5.2   Grade Distributions

The treatment group had a total of 73.8% students that successfully passed the course. Of the students that were not successful, 9.2% withdrew from the course (not included in the histogram) and 16.9% of students received a "D" or an "F" for the course. The grade distribution for the treatment group is shown in Figure 5.1.

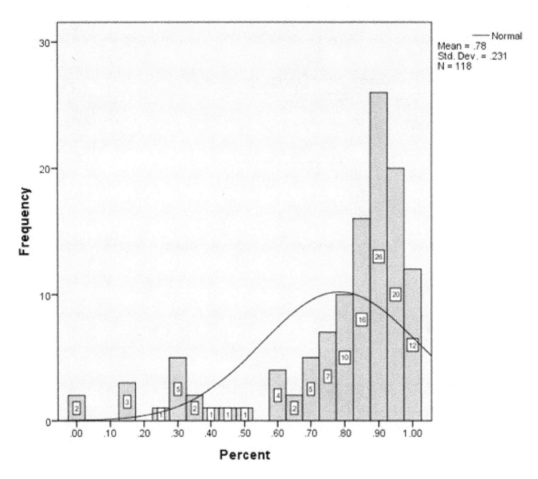

Figure 5.1 Histogram of grade distribution for treatment group.

The control group had a total of 68% students that successfully passed the course. Of the students that were not successful, 7.8% withdrew from the course (not included in the histogram) and 24.2% of students received a "D" or an "F" for the course. This yielded a 5.8% difference between the success rates of the treatment group (higher) versus the success rates of the control group. Figure 5.2 shows the grade distribution for the control group.

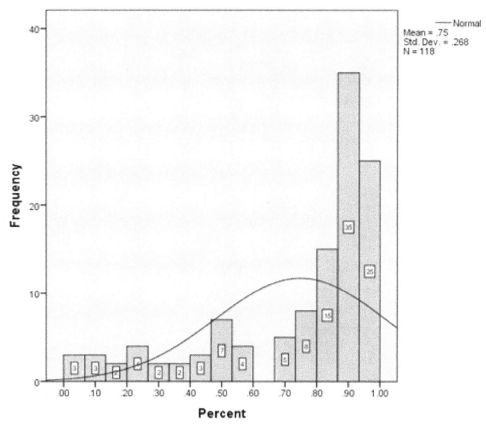

Figure 5.2. Histogram of grade distribution for control group.

The grade distributions for the Fundamentals of Programming course did not result in a normal distribution. There were a high number of As and Bs and the other grades were varied. The percentages ranged from 0 to 100%. The treatment group had a higher lower quartile than the control group. The minimum, excluding outliers, was much higher with the treatment group. Figure 5.3 features a boxplot of course percentages.

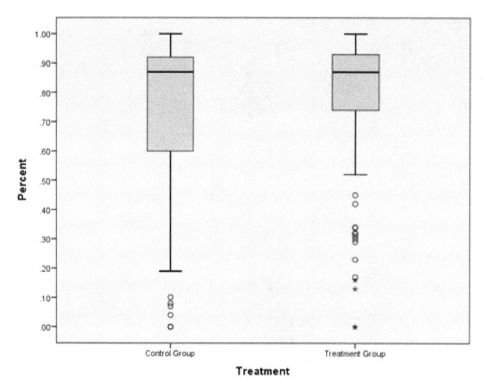

Figure 5.3. Course percentage comparison boxplot.

5.3   Reliability of Instrument

Cronbach's alpha was used to measure reliability of the instruments used for this study.

This type of analysis measures scales for internal consistency by measuring correlation of items

to determine reliability (Huck, 2004). There were seven journal entries given throughout the

course. The first journal entry included demographic information and measured starting

confidence levels for each of the programming concepts. Journals 2 through 7 were comprised of

qualitative and quantitative questions. The qualitative questions were geared towards time

management, challenges, perceptions, and knowledge. This qualitative data were used to

examine individual case studies. The quantitative questions measured self-efficacy and

perceptions of the Alice software throughout the course. The reliability of Journals 2 through 7

were tested for the quantitation portion, but were split into two scales: one for self-efficacy and one for Alice perceptions. Quantitative questions were Likert scales ratings from 1 (*low*) to 5 (*high*).

The starting confidence levels for the following programming concepts: variables, objects, classes, procedures, functions, parameters, conditionals, loops, and arrays as well as programming as a whole were measured at the beginning of the course. The reliability of this scale was tested and it had a Cronbach's alpha of 0.97 for these ten items. This alpha was considered excellent according to George and Mallery (2003) meaning that the internal consistency of the scale was high.

At the end of the course the students were asked to rate their understanding of each of the concepts. These concepts, 10 items, were tested and had Cronbach's alpha reliability of 0.96. This alpha verifies that this scale was highly reliable for measuring self-efficacy levels of using and understanding each of the concepts.

Student perceptions of Alice were measured at the end of the course. The participants were asked whether they found Alice to be useful, engaging, and intuitive overall. They were also asked to rate how much Alice helped them learn each concept (variables, objects, classes, procedures, functions, parameters, conditionals, loops, arrays, and programming as a whole). This scale had a total of 13 items with a Cronbach's alpha of 0.97, which means that the items on the scale were exceedingly consistent.

5.4 Impact of Self-Efficacy on Course Success

Multiple regression analysis was used to test if the final confidence ratings significantly predicted final course grades. The results of the regression indicated the 10 predictors explained 20% of the variance $(R^2 = 0.20, F(10,175) = 4.45, p < .001)$. It was found that confidence with conditionals statistically significantly predicted course success (β = *0.28, p* = .052), as did arrays (β = 0.36, *p* = .002). Table 5.13 presents the self-efficacy coefficients that should predict successful student completion of the course.

Table 5.13

Coefficients of Self-Efficacy in Predicting Course Success

Model	Unstandardized Coefficients		Standardized Coefficients	*t*	*p*
	β	Standard Error	β		
(Constant)	1.85	0.35		5.28	0.00
Variables	0.23	0.13	0.21	1.81	0.07
Objects	0.05	0.19	0.04	0.26	0.80
Classes	-0.25	0.18	-0.23	-1.37	0.17
Procedures	-0.17	0.15	-0.15	-1.12	0.26
Functions	-0.07	0.14	-0.06	-0.46	0.64
Parameters	0.05	0.11	0.05	0.47	0.64
Conditionals	0.31	0.14	0.31	2.22	0.28
Loops	-0.14	0.12	-0.15	-1.22	0.22
Arrays	0.36	0.12	0.37	3.11	0.00
Programming	-0.01	0.14	-0.00	-0.54	1.00

5.5   Correlations between Demographic Variables

Bivariate correlation analysis was used to determine if there were any associations among the demographic variables: gender, ethnicity, age, status, number of credits earned, class type, semester, prior programming experience, and major. There was a low degree of positive correlation between the age of the student and the type of class (afternoon, online, and evening) for which they registered, *r* = 0.251, *p* < .001; the older students were more likely to take online and evening courses. There was a small positive correlation between the age of the student and the credits which they completed thus far, $r = 0.268$, $p < .001$; the older students were more likely to have completed more credits. There was a weak positive correlation between the age of the student and their status, $r = 0.208$, $p = .001$; the older students were more likely to be part-time. The type of class that the students chose to take and the number of credits they have completed were slightly positively correlated, $r = 0.211$, $p = .001$; the online and evening students were more likely to have completed more credits. Correlation coefficients can be categorized as high (close to 1), moderate (mid-range), or weak (close to 0) according to Huck (2004). Table 5.14 shows the correlations between the demographic variables.

Table 5.14

Bivariate Correlations between Demographic Variables

Subscale		1	2	3	4	5	6	7	8	9
1. Ethnicity	Pearson r	--	.083	-.067	-.129*	-.098	.005	.075	-.071	-.016
	Sig. (2-tailed)		.186	.283	.039	.115	.942	.232	.259	.793
2. Gender	Pearson r		--	.149*	.005	-.050	.112	.018	-.130*	.054
	Sig. (2-tailed)			.017	.940	.420	.073	.776	.037	.392
3. Age	Pearson r			--	.208**	.251**	.268**	-.025	.004	-.157*
	Sig. (2-tailed)				.001	.000	.000	.691	.947	.012
4. Status	Pearson r				--	.125*	.175**	.003	.048	-.038
	Sig. (2-tailed)					.045	.005	.967	.446	.543
5. Time	Pearson r					--	.211**	-.025	.056	-.004
	Sig. (2-tailed)						.001	.694	.374	.944
6. Credits	Pearson r						--	-.033	-.060	.130*
	Sig. (2-tailed)							.596	.339	.037
7. Semester	Pearson r							--	-.014	-.138*
	Sig. (2-tailed)								.820	.027
8. Experience	Pearson r								--	-.007
	Sig. (2-tailed)									.912
9. Major	Pearson r									--
	Sig. (2-tailed)									

*. Correlation is significant at the 0.05 level (2-tailed).

**. Correlation is significant at the 0.01 level (2-tailed).

5.6   Testing Hypotheses

A one-way analysis of variance (ANOVA) was used to test the hypotheses: the success and confidence growth differences between the control and treatment group, measure the effect of demographics on confidence growth and success, and to determine the impact of demographics on Alice impressions. This statistical approach was used because of its ability to compare means between two groups (treatment and control) to determine significance (Huck, 2004). An alpha level of 0.05 was used for all ANOVA tests.

5.6.1   Control versus Treatment Group

The treatment group ($M = 2.54$, $SD = 1.10$) had statistically significantly higher confidence levels than the control group ($M = 2.20$, $SD = 1.29$) for procedures [$F(1, 184) = 3.83$, $p = .052$]. The treatment group produced a relatively small effect size of 0.14 (Cohen 1992). There were no statistically significant differences between the control and treatment groups for any of the other programming concepts. The treatment group had a higher average mean for the following concepts: objects, classes, procedures, functions, conditionals, and programming overall. Table 5.15 displays the mean and standard deviations for the control and treatment group for each programming concept.

Table 5.15

Control versus Treatment Group for Programming Growth

	Control Group (n=86)		Treatment Group (n=100)	
	Mean	SD	Mean	SD
Programming Growth	1.99	1.10	2.10	0.98
Variables Growth	2.29	1.31	2.20	1.21
Objects Growth	2.24	1.25	2.28	1.15
Classes Growth	2.29	1.15	2.29	1.26
Procedures Growth	2.20	1.29	2.54	1.10
Functions Growth	2.01	1.27	2.19	1.13
Parameters Growth	2.24	1.29	2.11	1.12
Conditionals Growth	2.22	1.34	2.28	1.04
Loops Growth	2.09	1.24	1.99	1.30
Arrays Growth	2.19	1.21	2.07	1.10

The assignment scores of the treatment group were higher and approaching statistical significance, $[F(1, 234) = 3.03, p = .083]$ with a small effect size of 0.12 (Cohen 1992). The treatment group had higher overall assignment scores, midterm scores, final scores, participation grade, percentages, and final grades. Table 5.16 shows the mean and standard deviations for the control versus the treatment group for course success.

Table 5.16

Control versus Treatment Group for Course Success

	Control Group			Treatment Group		
	n	Mean	*SD*	*n*	Mean	*SD*
Assignment Score	118	0.72	0.30	118	0.79	0.28
Midterm Exam	118	0.72	0.24	118	0.73	0.22
Final Exam	118	0.66	0.33	118	0.70	0.28
Participation Score	118	0.82	0.30	118	0.88	0.27
Course Percentage	118	0.75	0.27	118	0.78	0.21
Course Grade	128	2.33	1.83	130	2.43	1.71

Note. The 22 students that withdrew from the course were only counted in the course grade since they were not given an opportunity to complete the course.

5.6.2 Demographics on Control versus Treatment Self-Efficacy and Success

5.6.2.1 Gender

The females in the treatment group had more confidence level growth that was statistically significant for the following areas: objects $[F(1, 47) = 8.33, p = .006]$, classes $[F(1, 47) = 8.33, p = .008]$, procedures $[F(1, 47) = 6.98, p = .011]$, loops $[F(1, 47) = 4.76, p = .034]$, and programming overall $[F(1, 47) = 4.37, p = .042]$, with the following concepts approaching statistical significance: variables $[F(1, 47) = 3.81, p = .057]$ and conditionals $[F(1, 47) = 3.38, p = .072]$. According to Cohen (1992), there was a medium degree of effect for the following concepts: variables, objects, classes, procedures, conditionals, and programming overall. The medium effect size for variables and conditionals indicates that statistical significance could be reached with a larger sample size. The function, parameter, loop, and array concepts had a small effect (Cohen 1992). There was no statistical significance with males in the treatment versus control group. Table 5.17 presents the mean, standard deviations, and the effect sizes of males and females in the control versus the treatment group for each programming concept. The

females in the treatment group had a higher mean than the control group for each concept area.

Table 5.17

Gender Control and Treatment Group Differences with Self-Efficacy

		Males Control $n = 65$ Treatment $n = 72$		Females Control $n = 21$ Treatment $n = 28$		
		Mean	SD	Mean	SD	r
Programming Growth	Control	2.04	1.10	1.81	1.12	0.28
	Treatment	1.99	1.01	2.39	0.83	
Variables Growth	Control	2.35	1.26	2.10	1.48	0.26
	Treatment	1.97	1.21	2.79	0.99	
Objects Growth	Control	2.35	1.23	1.90	1.30	0.38
	Treatment	2.08	1.20	2.79	0.83	
Classes Growth	Control	2.40	1.28	1.95	1.16	0.37
	Treatment	2.31	1.18	2.82	1.02	
Procedures Growth	Control	2.28	1.24	1.95	1.16	0.39
	Treatment	2.43	1.16	2.82	0.86	
Functions Growth	Control	2.05	1.27	1.90	1.30	0.19
	Treatment	2.13	1.14	2.36	1.13	
Parameters Growth	Control	2.34	1.25	1.95	1.40	0.17
	Treatment	2.01	1.18	2.36	0.95	
Conditionals Growth	Control	2.34	1.34	1.86	1.31	0.25
	Treatment	2.21	1.05	2.46	1.00	
Loops Growth	Control	2.25	1.28	1.62	1.02	0.30
	Treatment	1.88	1.36	2.29	1.08	
Arrays Growth	Control	2.27	1.19	1.90	1.26	0.20
	Treatment	1.96	1.14	2.36	0.95	

Females in the treatment group scored statistically significantly higher on their

assignments [$F(1, 56) = 5.52, p = .022$], on their final exam [$F(1, 56) = 4.00, p = .050$], for their

participation grade [$F(1, 56) = 4.15, p = .046$], and in their overall percentage for the course

[$F(1, 56) = 4.19, p = .045$]. When withdrawals were factored into the final grades, the females in the treatment group still did statistically significantly better in the course [$F(1, 61) = 3.85, p = .054$]. Since the students who withdrew were not present for the entire course, they were not counted in the assignment scores, exam scores, participation scores, and course percentages; the withdrawn students only appear in the final grades section. There was a medium degree of effect with assignment, final exam, participation, and overall course scores (Cohen, 1992). The midterm exam scores and final grade in the course had a small effect (Cohen, 1992). There was no statistical significance with males in the treatment versus control group. The mean, standard deviation, and effect size for males and females in the control versus treatment group for course success are shown in Table 5.18. The females in the treatment group had a higher mean than the control group for each achievement milestone.

Table 5.18

Gender Control and Treatment Group Differences with Course Success

		Males			Females			
		n	Mean	*SD*	*n*	Mean	*SD*	*r*
Assignment Score	Control	90	0.72	0.28	28	0.72	0.34	0.29
	Treatment	88	0.75	0.30	30	0.89	0.21	
Midterm Exam	Control	90	0.72	0.24	28	0.72	0.24	0.10
	Treatment	88	0.72	0.24	30	0.76	0.15	
Final Exam	Control	90	0.67	0.33	28	0.63	0.36	0.25
	Treatment	88	0.67	0.32	30	0.77	0.11	
Participation Score	Control	90	0.82	0.28	28	0.81	0.35	0.27
	Treatment	88	0.85	0.30	30	0.96	0.16	
Course Percentage	Control	90	0.75	0.26	28	0.74	0.31	0.25
	Treatment	88	0.76	0.25	30	0.86	0.12	
Course Grade	Control	96	2.38	1.80	32	2.19	1.94	0.24
	Treatment	99	2.25	1.80	31	3.00	1.27	

Note. The 22 students that withdrew from the course were only counted in the course grade since they were not given an opportunity to complete the course.

To determine if there was an overall difference between gender and confidence growth, an ANOVA was conducted with both groups combined and no statistically significant differences were found. Overall males had a higher starting confidence level mean for each programming concept, but were only statistically significant in the following areas: variables $[F(1, 256) = 6.93, p = .009]$, objects $[F(1, 256) = 4.58, p = .033]$, functions $[F(1, 256) = 4.12, p = .044]$, parameters $[F(1, 256) = 5.98, p = .015]$, and loops $[F(1, 256) = 4.11, p = .044]$. Table 5.19 depicts the differences with starting confidence levels based on gender.

Table 5.19

Differences with Starting Self-Efficacy Levels and Gender

	Males ($n = 195$)		Females ($n = 63$)	
	Mean	SD	Mean	SD
Programming Overall	1.69	0.94	1.44	0.71
Variables	2.08	1.24	1.62	1.08
Objects	1.84	1.10	1.51	0.91
Classes	1.73	1.05	1.48	0.86
Procedures	1.65	0.99	1.44	0.86
Functions	1.88	1.07	1.57	1.03
Parameters	1.69	1.02	1.35	0.77
Conditionals	1.72	1.03	1.46	0.93
Loops	1.89	1.19	1.56	1.00
Arrays	1.60	0.92	1.40	0.81

5.6.2.2 Ethnicity

The Asian students in the treatment group ($n = 19$, $M = 0.97$, $SD = 0.12$) had statistically significantly higher rate of participation than the control group ($n = 18$, $M = 0.78$, $SD = 0.32$), $[F(1, 35) = 5.62, p = .023]$. There was no statistically significant difference of confidence growth between the treatment and control groups for various ethnicities.

5.6.2.3 Age

The 18-21 year old students in the treatment group ($n = 37$, $M = 2.11$, $SD = 1.22$) had statistically significantly lower level of growth for variables than the control group ($n = 30$, $M = 2.70$, $SD = 0.95$), [$F(1, 35) = 4.72$, $p = .033$]. The 22-29 year old students in the treatment group had statistically significantly higher scores than the control group on their assignments [$F(1, 88) = 13.21$, $p < .001$], their final exams [$F(1, 88) = 3.87$, $p = .052$], their participation points [$F(1, 88) = 7.90$, $p = .006$], and their percentage in the course [$F(1, 88) = 7.23$, $p = .009$]. There was a medium effect on assignment, final exam, and overall scores in the course, while the course grade had a small effect (Cohen, 1992), as shown in Table 5.20.

Table 5.20

Success Differences for 22-29 Year Old Students in Treatment versus Control Groups

	Control Group			Treatment Group			r
	n	Mean	SD	n	Mean	SD	
Assignment Score	49	0.62	0.33	41	0.85	0.26	0.36
Midterm Exam	49	0.69	0.27	41	0.71	0.24	0.04
Final Exam	49	0.56	0.39	41	0.70	0.26	0.20
Participation Score	49	0.73	0.36	41	0.90	0.23	0.27
Course Percentage	49	0.66	0.29	41	0.81	0.23	0.28
Course Grade	54	1.80	1.94	47	2.47	1.78	0.18

Note. The 11 students that withdrew from the course were only counted in the course grade since they were not given an opportunity to complete the course.

5.6.2.4 Status (Full-Time or Part-Time)

There was no statistically significant difference of success or confidence growth between the treatment and control groups for full-time or part-time students.

5.6.2.5 Number of Credits Earned

The students that took more than 60 credits in the treatment group ($n = 24$, $M = 0.94$, $SD = 0.17$) had statistically significantly higher rate of participation than the control group ($n = 22$, $M = 0.77$, $SD = 0.33$), [$F(1, 44) = 5.15$, $p = .028$]. There was no statistically significant difference in course success between the treatment and control groups based on the number of credit hours that a student has completed.

5.6.2.6 Class Type (Afternoon, Evening, Online)

The treatment group ($n = 52$, $M = 0.94$, $SD = 0.18$) students who had taken the afternoon class had statistically significantly higher rate of participation than the control group ($n = 55$, $M = 0.82$, $SD = 0.32$), [$F(1, 105) = 6.00$, $p = .016$]. The online and night students in the treatment and control groups did not vary enough to be considered statistically significant.

The students that took the class in the afternoon in the treatment group ($n = 52$, $M = 2.89$, $SD = 0.86$) had statistically significantly higher confidence growth for procedures than the control group ($n = 55$, $M = 2.39$, $SD = 1.26$), [$F(1, 84) = 4.66$, $p = .034$]. There was no statistically significant difference of confidence growth between the treatment and control groups for the online and night students.

5.6.2.7 Prior Programming Experience

The participants were grouped into two categories based on their experience level. The students with no programming experience or only HTML experience were categorized as having "no experience". The students with scripting experience and/or experience with at least one programming language were counted as the "experience" group and accounted for 54.3%.

The students that did not have prior programming experience in the treatment group (n = 57, M = 0.81, SD = 0.28) had statistically significantly higher assignment scores than the control group (n = 52, M = 0.68, SD = 0.31), [$F(1, 107)$ = 5.59, p = .020]. There was no statistically significant difference between the treatment and control groups with regards to prior programming experience and confidence growth with programming concepts.

5.6.2.8 Major

The participants were grouped into three categories of majors. The computer science majors accounted for 55%, math and engineering majors were comprised of 24%, and the remaining 21% were all other majors. The computer science majors in the treatment group had a statistically significantly higher level of growth than the control group for the following concepts: classes [$F(1, 99)$ = 6.73, p = .011], procedures [$F(1, 99)$ = 6.12, p = .015], functions [$F(1, 99)$ = 3.83, p = .053], and programming overall [$F(1, 99)$ = 4.44, p = .038]. The treatment group had a higher growth mean for each programming concept. There was a medium effect with the concept of classes and a small effect size with the following concepts: objects, procedures, functions, conditionals, and programming overall (Cohen 1992). Although objects and conditionals were not statistically significant, the effect size indicates that they may become significant with a larger sample size. The differences between the control and treatment computer science majors are indicated in Table 5.21. The computer science majors in the treatment group had a higher mean than the control group for each concept area.

The other majors did not have a statistically significant difference between the control and treatment group with confidence level growth. There was no statistically significant difference with course success between the treatment and control groups and choice of major.

Table 5.21

Self-Efficacy Growth for Computer Science Majors in Treatment versus Control Groups

	Control Group (n = 41)		Treatment Group (n = 60)		r
	Mean	SD	Mean	SD	
Programming Growth	1.61	1.09	2.07	1.06	0.21
Variables Growth	1.95	1.47	2.20	1.19	0.09
Objects Growth	1.95	1.36	2.30	1.11	0.14
Classes Growth	1.85	1.30	2.48	1.13	0.25
Procedures Growth	1.85	1.41	2.48	1.14	0.24
Functions Growth	1.61	1.32	2.10	1.17	0.19
Parameters Growth	1.98	1.39	2.02	1.07	0.02
Conditionals Growth	1.90	1.53	2.22	1.06	0.12
Loops Growth	1.76	1.24	1.97	1.30	0.08
Arrays Growth	1.83	1.26	2.02	1.05	0.08

The computer science majors in both groups had less growth in confidence than the other majors, but they also started with a higher confidence level for all areas. Computer science majors include: programming, computer information systems, web programming, and gaming. Table 5.22 shows the self-efficacy growth for computer science, math and engineering, and all other majors.

Table 5.22

Self-Efficacy Growth for Various Majors

	Computer Science (n = 101)		Math and Engineering (n = 46)		Other (n = 39)	
	Mean	SD	Mean	SD	Mean	SD
Programming Growth	1.88	1.09	2.30	0.92	2.18	0.97
Variables Growth	2.20	1.31	2.48	1.01	2.33	1.34
Objects Growth	2.16	1.22	2.48	0.98	2.28	1.34
Classes Growth	2.23	1.23	2.63	0.93	2.46	1.39
Procedures Growth	2.23	1.29	2.70	0.96	2.41	1.16
Functions Growth	1.90	1.25	2.39	1.06	2.31	1.13
Parameters Growth	2.00	1.20	2.37	1.16	2.38	1.23
Conditionals Growth	2.09	1.27	2.41	1.05	2.49	1.05
Loops Growth	1.88	1.28	2.33	1.10	2.10	1.41
Arrays Growth	1.94	1.14	2.37	1.00	2.31	1.30

5.6.2.9. Semester

The spring 2012 semester treatment group ($n = 40$, $M = 2.88$, $SD = 1.07$) had more confidence level growth for procedures than the control group ($n = 46$, $M = 2.24$, $SD = 1.32$), [$F(1, 84) = 5.92$, $p = .017$].

5.6.3   Demographics on Alice impressions

5.6.3.1. Gender

Statistically, females found Alice to be more engaging [$F(1, 98) = 20.23$, $p < .001$], intuitive [$F(1, 98) = 8.12$, $p = .005$], and useful [$F(1, 98) = 22.81$, $p < .001$] than males. Females rated Alice statistically significantly higher for its ability to teach variables [$F(1, 98) = 5.01$, $p = .027$], objects [$F(1, 98) = 6.55$, $p = .012$], classes [$F(1, 98) = 10.50$, $p = .002$], procedures [$F(1, 98) = 9.63$, $p = .003$], functions [$F(1, 98) = 12.15$, $p = .001$], parameters [$F(1, 98) = 14.05$, $p < .001$], conditionals [$F(1, 98) = 6.39$, $p = .013$], loops [$F(1, 98) = 6.32$, $p = .014$], and arrays [$F(1, 98) = 10.41$, $p = .002$]. Females rated the usefulness of each programming concept higher than males. According to Cohen (1992), this would indicate that there was a large degree of effect on females with their perception of the usefulness of the software to teach programming concepts and engagement factor of the software. Table 5.23 shows the Alice impression differences between males and females.

Table 5.23

Alice Impressions for Gender

	Males (n = 72)		Females (n = 28)		r
	Mean	SD	Mean	SD	
Teaching Concepts	3.13	1.21	4.32	0.86	0.49
Engaging	3.35	1.41	4.61	0.74	0.49
Intuitive	3.74	1.22	4.46	0.92	0.32
Teaching Variables	3.28	1.31	3.89	0.99	0.25
Teaching Objects	3.60	1.33	4.29	0.81	0.30
Teaching Classes	3.38	1.31	4.25	0.93	0.36
Teaching Procedures	3.28	1.28	4.11	0.96	0.34
Teaching Functions	3.26	1.25	4.18	0.98	0.38
Teaching Parameters	3.10	1.26	4.14	0.93	0.43
Teaching Conditionals	3.13	1.30	3.82	1.06	0.28
Teaching Loops	2.97	1.32	3.68	1.09	0.28
Teaching Arrays	2.75	1.34	3.68	1.16	0.35

5.6.3.2. Class Type (Afternoon, Evening, Online)

Overall there was no statistical significant difference between the type of class (face-to-face afternoon, face-to-face evening, or online) and the perceived intuitiveness, usefulness, and excitement level of the Alice environment, but the online classes had a higher mean for each of these areas. When comparing individual concepts, only two concepts were statistically significant: loops [$F(2, 97) = 3.07, p = .051$] and arrays [$F(2, 97) = 3.19, p = .045$]. The impressions of the Alice environment by class type are revealed in Table 5.24.

Table 5.24

Alice Impressions by Class Type

	Afternoon (n = 45)		Night (n = 35)		Online (n = 20)	
	Mean	SD	Mean	SD	Mean	SD
Teaching Concepts	3.42	1.34	3.20	1.28	3.66	1.08
Engaging	3.58	1.45	3.45	1.47	4.00	1.19
Intuitive	3.91	1.20	3.65	1.42	4.14	1.00
Teaching Variables	3.36	1.33	3.20	1.32	3.71	1.10
Teaching Objects	3.78	1.33	3.50	1.38	3.97	1.04
Teaching Classes	3.53	1.31	3.30	1.42	3.91	1.10
Teaching Procedures	3.44	1.32	3.40	1.31	3.66	1.14
Teaching Functions	3.49	1.36	3.30	1.22	3.69	1.11
Teaching Parameters	3.42	1.44	2.90	1.25	3.63	1.19
Teaching Conditionals	3.22	1.30	3.00	1.38	3.63	1.14
Teaching Loops	3.04	1.31	2.75	1.25	3.57	1.22
Teaching Arrays	2.82	1.37	2.65	1.42	3.46	1.20

5.6.3.3 Prior Programming Experience

There was a statistically significant difference between the prior programming experience of the student and their feelings towards the Alice environment. Overall the less experienced students found Alice to be more useful [$F(1, 98) = 6.13, p = .015, r = 0.24$], engaging [$F(1, 98) = 4.29, p = .041, r = 0.20$], and more intuitive [$F(1, 98) = 3.52, p = .064, r = 0.18$]. The less experienced students also rated the usefulness of Alice higher for each individual concept, but this difference was not statistically significant. The Alice impressions varied by experience level as shown in Table 5.34.

Table 5.34

Alice Impressions by Experience Level

	No Experience (n =50)		Experience (n = 50)	
	Mean	SD	Mean	SD
Teaching Concepts	3.76	1.12	3.16	1.30
Engaging	3.98	1.20	3.42	1.49
Intuitive	4.16	1.04	3.72	1.29
Teaching Variables	3.58	1.03	3.32	1.45
Teaching Objects	3.90	1.11	3.68	1.36
Teaching Classes	3.68	1.15	3.56	1.39
Teaching Procedures	3.68	1.10	3.34	1.38
Teaching Functions	3.70	1.09	3.34	1.36
Teaching Parameters	3.56	1.18	3.22	1.46
Teaching Conditionals	3.50	1.17	3.14	1.36
Teaching Loops	3.28	1.25	3.06	1.35
Teaching Arrays	3.24	1.24	2.78	1.43

5.6.3.4 Major

The computer science majors had a higher mean rating for the perceived usefulness and engagement level of the Alice environment, but this did not reach significance. When examining individual concepts, the computer science majors had a higher mean that was statistically significant for parameters $[F(2, 97) = 3.25, p = .043]$. The means and standard deviations by major are presented in Table 5.26.

Table 5.26

Alice Impressions by Major

	Computer Science (*n* = 45)		Math and Engineering (*n* = 35)		Other Majors (*n* = 20)	
	Mean	*SD*	Mean	*SD*	Mean	*SD*
Teaching Concepts	3.57	1.21	3.32	1.29	3.29	1.31
Engaging	3.80	1.33	3.53	1.39	3.57	1.54
Intuitive	3.97	1.18	3.68	1.25	4.10	1.18
Teaching Variables	3.60	1.21	3.42	1.39	3.05	1.24
Teaching Objects	3.92	1.18	3.84	1.30	3.38	1.32
Teaching Classes	3.73	1.23	3.79	1.27	3.14	1.32
Teaching Procedures	3.70	1.18	3.37	1.34	3.10	1.30
Teaching Functions	3.72	1.18	3.42	1.31	3.05	1.28
Teaching Parameters	3.65	1.27	3.16	1.34	2.86	1.20
Teaching Conditionals	3.48	1.23	3.32	1.42	2.86	1.20
Teaching Loops	3.27	1.31	3.26	1.33	2.81	1.21
Teaching Arrays	3.10	1.36	3.11	1.37	2.67	1.32

5.6.3.5 Semester

When examining individual concepts, the spring 2012 students had a higher mean for loops [$F(1, 98) = 3.80, p = .054, r = 0.19$] and arrays [$F(1, 98) = 4.36, p = 0.039, r = 0.21$] that was statistically significant. The semester means and standard deviations for Alice impressions are listed in Table 5.27.

Table 5.27

Alice Impressions by Semester

	Spring 2012 (*n* = 40)		Fall 2012 (*n* = 60)	
	Mean	SD	Mean	SD
Teaching Concepts	3.45	1.40	3.47	1.14
Engaging	3.75	1.43	3.67	1.35
Intuitive	3.95	1.22	3.93	1.18
Teaching Variables	3.45	1.30	3.45	1.24
Teaching Objects	3.78	1.27	3.80	1.23
Teaching Classes	3.58	1.32	3.65	1.25
Teaching Procedures	3.55	1.34	3.48	1.20
Teaching Functions	3.55	1.32	3.50	1.20
Teaching Parameters	3.50	1.43	3.32	1.27
Teaching Conditionals	3.40	1.36	3.27	1.22
Teaching Loops	3.48	1.38	2.97	1.21
Teaching Arrays	3.35	1.29	2.78	1.35

5.6.3.5 Other Demographic Variables with No Significance

The following demographic variables did not have statistically significant differences with their perceptions of the Alice environment: age, ethnicity, student status, and number of credits earned.

5.6.4   Summary

The instrumentation for this study was found to be exceptionally reliable. Self-efficacy can predict 20% of the final course grade. The treatment group had a higher mean for assignment scores, midterm scores, final scores, participation grades, course percentages, course grades, and the following programming concepts: objects, classes, procedures, functions, conditionals, and programming overall, but only procedures and the final exam scores were statistically significant.

When comparing females in the treatment group and control group, the treatment group scored statistically significantly higher on their assignments, final exam, participation grade, overall percentage for the course, course grade including withdraws and had a statistically significant difference in confidence growth for the following areas: objects, classes, procedures, loops, and programming overall, with the following concepts approaching statistical significance: variables and conditionals. The Asian students in the treatment group had statistically significantly higher rate of participation than the control group. The 18-21 year old students in the treatment group had statistically significantly lower level of growth for variables than the control group. The 22-29 year old students in the treatment group had statistically significantly higher scores than the control group on their assignments, their final exams, their participation points, and their percentage in the course. The treatment group students who had taken the afternoon class had statistically significantly higher rates of participation and higher confidence growth for procedures than the control group. The students who did not have prior programming experience in the treatment group had statistically significantly higher assignment scores than the control group. The computer science majors in the treatment group had a statistically significantly higher level of growth than the control group for the following concepts: classes, procedures, functions, and programming overall. The treatment group had a higher growth mean for each programming concept, but it was not statistically significant. The spring 2012 semester treatment group had more confidence level growth for procedures than the control group.

Females rated Alice higher for engagement, intuitiveness, and usefulness; this was found to be statistically significant. The online students found Alice to be statistically significantly more worthwhile for teaching looping and arrays; they also found Alice to be more intuitive, useful, and exciting than the face-to-face classes, but this was not statistically significant. The less experienced students found Alice to be statistically significantly more useful, engaging, and intuitive. Computer science majors rated the usefulness of Alice to be statistically significantly higher for parameters, and they rated it the highest for engagement, but it was not statistically significant. The spring 2012 students found Alice to be statistically more significant for learning looping and array concepts.

CHAPTER 6

QUALITATIVE RESULTS

The qualitative results presented here are used to provide context for the quantitative results. There were a total of 130 participants in the treatment group, however only 96 of those students sufficiently completed the qualitative sections of the journals. The 34 students who were not included in the qualitative results were due to nonexistent or insufficient answers such as, "I don't know." Of those 34 students, one received an A for the course, two received Bs, one received a C, fourteen received Fs, and twelve received Ws.

6.1   Codes, Categories, and Themes

The journal entries for the 96 students were transferred into text documents and uploaded to Dedoose[22], qualitative research analysis software. After rereading the journal entries several times, the entries were broken down into descriptive codes. These codes were used to construct categories (Merriam, 2009). The categories were created based upon the positive and negative reactions to the Alice environment. Finally, themes were created based on the frequency and relationship of the codes and categories. The codes, categories, and themes were compared by two other researchers to create inter-rater reliability. The themes were quotes taken directly from the participants. The creation of codes, grouping of codes into categories, and generation of theories (themes) was based on Robson's (2002) systematic approach to analyzing qualitative data.

- The Alice environment is useful in demonstrating most Java concepts, but cannot be used to demonstrate them all.

---

[22] SocioCultural Research Consultants, http://www.dedoose.com

- I am a beginner programmer and it is easier to make the connection to "writing" code when you can actually build it, manipulate it, and see it taking form in an animated environment.
- I am not a fan of Alice. I have a lot of programming experience so I'd much rather dive right into the syntax.
- It is very easy to use and can be very fun and engaging.
- I find it to be clunky and buggy, and while the basic idea to get users accustomed to object-oriented programming is good, it's just too much of a pain to implement complex movements or any sort of mathematical operation.

The categories emerged from the descriptive codes: advantages and disadvantages of Alice design, cognitive benefits and disadvantages of Alice, and positive and negative general attitudes toward Alice. The qualitative categories that emerged from the descriptive codes validated the quantitative Likert scale where users rated how easy it was to use the software, how useful they felt it was for teaching those programming concepts, and how much they enjoyed using the Alice environment.

Table 6.1 listed the advantages of the Alice software design.

Table 6.1

Advantages with Alice Design

Code	Frequency	Head Count
Easy to use	83	38
Comfortable with environment	25	19
Easy to understand	18	15
No worrying about syntax	4	3
Well designed	3	2

The cognitive benefits of using the Alice software are shown in Table 6.2.

Table 6.2

Cognitive Benefits of Alice

Code	Frequency	Head Count
Useful way to introduce programming	78	44
Makes concepts easier to understand	52	35
Helps visual learners	52	27
Makes code easier to understand	28	17
Different way to learn code	7	5
Transferring Alice to Java code helps	6	3

Table 6.3 lists the general positive attitudes of using the Alice environment.

Table 6.3

Positive General Attitudes Toward Alice

Code	Frequency	Head Count
Enjoyable	87	44
Interesting/Entertaining/Engaging	33	20
Prefer Alice over pure Java coding	17	11
Interactive	12	8
Allows for creativity	6	5

The disadvantages of the Alice software design are listed in Table 6.4.

Table 6.4

Disadvantages of Alice Design

Code	Frequency	Head Count
Technical problems	43	22
Interface is restricting	14	10
Limited models	7	5
Lack of Alice resources	6	2
Too much time setting up scene	3	3

Table 6.5 lists the cognitive disadvantage of using Alice.

Table 6.5

Cognitive Disadvantages of Alice

Code	Frequency	Head Count
Alice is not good for all concepts	23	16
Inappropriate for level of student	21	10
Alice confuses me	20	15
Learned more by pure coding	15	11
Did not improve skills	14	10
More work learning another environment	4	3
Generated Java Code from Alice is hard to decipher	3	3

The general negative attitudes towards the Alice environment are listed in Table 6.6.

Table 6.6

Negative General Attitudes Toward Alice

Code	Frequency	Head Count
Prefer typing code instead of drag and drop environment	43	25
Boring	8	5

6.2   Case Studies

The students were asked to complete seven journal entries throughout the course. These journal entries contained quantitative and qualitative questions. The qualitative questions were used to gain insight into the quantitative data. One student was chosen to represent each of the themes gathered from the qualitative data. The case studies were chosen based on demographics to be representative of the sample population. The student names were changed to protect confidentiality. Table 6.7 lists the selected case study participant demographics.

Table 6.7

Participants Selected for Case Studies

	Gender	Ethnicity	Age Range	Major	Experience Level	Class Type	Semester
Ana	Female	Hispanic	18-21	Engineering	No Experience	Evening	Fall 2012
Amy	Female	Caucasian	25-29	Undecided	Little Experience	Online	Spring 2012
Steve	Male	Caucasian	30-39	Comp. Sci.	Experienced	Online	Spring 2012
George	Male	Caucasian	Over 50	Comp. Sci.	Some Experience	Afternoon	Spring 2012
Sam	Male	Asian	18-21	Comp. Sci.	Some Experience	Evening	Fall 2012

One participant was chosen to represent each theme. The participants and their associated theme are listed in Table 6.8.

Table 6.8

Student and Associated Theme

Name	Theme
Ana	The Alice environment is useful in demonstrating most Java concepts, but cannot be used to demonstrate them all.
Amy	It is very easy to use and can be very fun and engaging.
Steve	I am not a fan of Alice. I have a lot of programming experience so I'd much rather dive right into the syntax.
George	I am a beginner programmer and it is easier to make the connection to "writing" code when you can actually build it, manipulate it, and see it taking form in an animated environment.
Sam	I find it to be clunky and buggy, and while the basic idea to get users accustomed to object-oriented programming is good, it's just too much of a pain to implement complex movements or any sort of mathematical operation.

6.3 Rich Descriptions of Student Participants

6.3.1. Ana

Ana was a geotechnical engineering student. She was in the 18-21 age range and of Hispanic descent. She was a full-time student enrolled in the fall 2012 semester evening treatment section. She did not have any prior programming experience. Ana had completed all of the exercises and assignments for the course and averaged an 87% on the midterm and final; she earned an "A" for the course. She took the course because she thought that it sounded interesting. This student started the course with a confidence level of 1 (lowest level) for each programming concept, but then increased her confidence level of to a 5 (highest level) for each concept by the end of the course. She rated Alice as a five for engagement, usefulness, and intuitiveness at the end of the course.

> I like the Alice environment a lot. I like that it already has models and is very easy to use. I can complete a project, which would be otherwise very difficult, somewhat quickly. I wish the "edit code" area was easier to read though, because the drop-down option tends to block the ends of a phrase. Other than that, I enjoy using the Alice environment for complex 3D projects.

> I love the Alice environment, because it allows me to get a visual of what I am doing. I also enjoy using NetBeans though, because it allows me to understand what I am doing more. Although the Alice environment was helpful in visually teaching programming objectives, there were times when NetBeans was the better option. For example, arrays were easier to understand through NetBeans. There were also times where I felt like Alice made it too easy to complete a task, because it consisted of finding buttons instead of typing out the entire code. But all in all, I believe the Alice environment was useful in teaching me java concepts.

6.3.2. Amy

Amy was undecided with her major. She was of Caucasian descent and was in the 25-29 age range. She was a part-time student with less than 15 credit hours. She only had HTML experience in high school. She was enrolled in the spring 2012 semester in the online treatment class. Amy had completed all of the exercises and assignments for the course. She averaged a 75% on the midterm and final and earned a "B" for the course. She took the course online because she had young children and needed to be home with them. This student started the course with a confidence level of one (lowest level) for each programming concept, then grew to a confidence level of five (highest level) for each concept by the end of the course. She also rated Alice a five for engagement, usefulness, and intuitiveness for each concept throughout the course.

> I like the Alice environment a lot. It's easy to use and very engaging. I prefer Alice to Netbeans. Alice really is a straight forward program. Each object has its own individual Method, Function, and Properties. You can create a 3D environment within a few hours, or a full game within a couple days. It's a very easy to use program and lets the designer's mind wonder endlessly. It is a great program for individuals wanting to learn how to create a program that does specific interactions by dragging and dropping the item to the programming board. It's a really easy to use programming environment that helps someone with no programming experience, feel comfortable and drawn into the learning environment that Alice creates.

6.3.3. Steve

Steve was in his thirties and of Caucasian descent. He was a part-time student majoring in computer science. Steve was enrolled in the spring 2012 semester in the online treatment class. He was proficient with other programming languages including: C, C++, Basic, Visual Basic, Pascal, Javascript, and other scripting languages. He took the class to learn Java. He completed all of the exercises and assignments for the course and averaged a 97% on the midterm and final and earned an "A" for the course. This student started and ended the course with a confidence level of a four for each programming concept. He rated Alice as a two for engagement and usefulness; he rated intuitiveness as a three.

> It's cute. For non-programmers, I think it's an excellent way to demonstrate the ideas presented in the text. It gives novice programmers the ability to see their code do

85

something more interesting than calculating interest or doing geometry work. That said, I feel like the Java parts of the reviews are more useful to me. It's good for beginning coders and people that haven't had to deal with "pure" data and logic much. For me, I'd rather just write a second Java program, but I don't think I'm really the target audience for this class, so that's okay. It's a good tool for engaging non-programmers, but is somewhat frustrating for me to work with, as so much of it is a mouse-click oriented UI instead of a text entry.

6.3.4. George

George was of Caucasian descent and from the 50-plus age group. He was a part-time student with more than 60 credit hours. His major was Computer Science and he had experience with Basic and FORTRAN. He was enrolled in the spring 2012 semester in the afternoon treatment class. George had completed all of the exercises and assignments for the course and averaged a 97% on the midterm and final and earned an "A" for the course. This student started the course with confidence levels ranging from one to four and ended the course with levels ranging from three to five for the programming concepts. He rated Alice as a four for usefulness and intuitiveness; he rated the environment engagement as a 5.

> It is a very good teaching method. I like to "see" concepts as I learn them. It is very helpful to get an understanding of the concepts of methods. I like it - makes things visual and easier to understand. It is a good visual tool to learn about programming. It helped me a lot.

6.3.5. Sam

Sam was an Asian male in the 18-21 age range. He was a full-time student majoring in computer science. He had prior Java experience in high school. Sam was enrolled in the fall 2012 semester in the evening treatment class. He had completed all of the exercises and assignments for the course and averaged a 98% on the midterm and final and earned an "A" for the course. This course was required for his major. This student started the course with a confidence level of a one or a two for each programming concept and ended up rating himself as a level three for each concept by the end of the course. This student ended up with a 99% in the course, but still did not feel confident in his programming ability. He rated Alice as a three for engagement, usefulness, and intuitiveness.

> It is straightforward and easy to use. However, it gets stuck sometimes, and I can't explore the environment, and so I have to exit Alice and again open it. This has happened about three times till now. Alice is sometimes useful, but sometimes it makes the concept more complex. Everytime I open Alice and set up my scene, I cannot resize or move around the objects. I have to restart it and then only can I do anything to the objects. This constantly happens. It is an effective way to learn the logic of coding without worrying about the hassles of syntax and the other difficulties of programming. It's pretty straightforward and simple to use. However, sometimes it hangs and that is really frustrating. I guess since this is the beta version, there are many more bugs that are being fixed.

6.4   Tutor Reactions

The tutors for this class have had experience with coding in Java and working with the Alice software. They were enrolled in Fundamentals of Programming and received an "A" in the course. The tutors were chosen because they were dedicated, hard-working, and intelligent individuals who were able to analyze difficult programming concepts and explain them to others.

6.4.1. Joe

Joe was a Caucasian male in his early thirties. He was a web development student going to school part-time while doing graphic design freelancing. This tutor was a student in the evening face-to-face Fundamentals of Programming class during the spring 2011 semester. He described the Alice environment as beneficial, because it offered students a way of "learning programming through an interactive media." He proceeded to explain why he felt that this environment was beneficial.

It allows students to experiment with programming in a safe and carefree environment and at the same time is teaching them. It offers students a new way to look at programming and how programming can be useful, meaningful, and fun. When a student begins learning programming it's easy to become concerned that the subject material is too difficult to learn, because of the complexity of the subject itself. With the Alice environment it breaks down the lines of code and opens up a world of imagination.

6.4.2. Bob

Bob was a Caucasian male and in his early twenties. He was an engineering student that transferred to a nearby university after two years of study at the community college. This tutor was a student in the face-to-face afternoon Fundamentals of Programming class during the spring 2011 semester. He enjoyed using the Alice environment and felt that it was a great tool for teaching Java fundamentals. The tutor believed that many students loved the concept of Alice and the visual aspects associated with it, but that some students were irritated with the bugs that came with using beta software.

Alice provides an alternative to programming fundamentals not typically found in a college setting. Rather than forcing students to memorize syntax and struggle with foreign definitions of things like variables and parameters, Alice allows the user to mess around with the code and see the results visually. I think once a number of the bugs are removed and an innovative way to handle drop-down box navigation is discovered, Alice will be a critical tool in building programming fundamentals for years to come.

6.4.3. Sue

Sue was of Asian descent and was in her late twenties. She had her master's degree in Educational Technology and worked as a part-time instructional technologist. She was taking web development courses to keep her skills up to date. This tutor was a student in the face-to-face afternoon Fundamentals of Programming class during the spring 2011 semester. She enjoyed using the Alice environment and believed that it was beneficial for students to work with visual objects in Alice to understand abstract programming and coding.

Java really clicked when Alice helped me to understand what a method is and how it works. The only thing that was difficult about Alice was navigating the 3D environment; trying to use the arrows to position your characters and objects.

6.4.4. John

John was in his early twenties and of Caucasian descent. He majored in Computer Science; he took classes at the college involved in this study and another nearby university. John attended the evening face-to-face Fundamentals of Programming class during the fall 2011 semester. He felt that the environment was a bit "cartoony" and preferred to type the code in an editor instead of using the drag and drop environment. He believed that the environment had bugs that need to be fixed, but felt that the environment had improved since he used it back in the beta stages of 2011. He indicated that it would be nice if Alice differentiated technical errors and user errors; it made it hard to debug Alice code without having more details about what is causing an error.

> I believe that Alice does have its place in teaching people some of the basics of coding without having to worry about the creation of new objects. I still believe that Alice is beneficial to the students because it helps break down concepts, although it does make some concepts a little bit more confusing I believe (Arrays) it still makes the majority of coding structure easier to understand due to the graphic interface.

6.4.5. Mary

Mary was in her thirties and of Indian descent. She had her Master's degree in Software Engineering from India. She decided to come back to school to pursue a certificate in mobile computing specifically in Android development. This tutor was a student in the afternoon face-to-face Fundamentals of Programming class during the fall 2011 semester. Although she had had prior programming experience and had her Master's degree in Software Engineering, she took the Fundamentals of Programming course to learn Java. She felt that many students enjoyed

using the Alice environment.

> It is very user friendly. Even a person without any programming experience can easily
> use this tool and create animations and games. Alice makes object oriented programming
> easy and fun, giving them an opportunity to show their creative side, along with their
> programming skills in Java.

CHAPTER 7

DISCUSSION

7.1   Emerging Themes and Qualitative Reactions

The emerging qualitative themes were chosen based upon the top level codes from each category. The codes are represented in italics and the themes are in quotations since they were quotes taken directly from students. The *easy to use* code was mentioned 83 times by 38 different students and *enjoyable* was stated 87 times by 44 people; these two codes were used to create the following theme: "It is very easy to use and can be very fun and engaging." The *useful way to introduce programming* was used 78 times by 44 people and was used to create the theme, "I am a beginner programmer and it is easier to make the connection to writing code when you can actually build it, manipulate it, and see it taking form in an animated environment." The *technical problems* mentioned 43 times by 22 students and the *interface is restricting* code stated 14 times by 10 students was used to create the following theme: "I find it to be clunky and buggy, and while the basic idea to get users accustomed to object-oriented programming is good, it's just too much of a pain to implement complex movements or any sort of mathematical operation." The *prefer typing code instead of working with the drag and drop environment* code was used 43 times by 25 students and the inappropriate for level of student code that was mentioned 21 times by 10 students were joined together to create the theme, "I am not a fan of Alice. I have a lot of programming experience so I'd much rather dive right into the syntax." The *Alice is not good for all concepts* code was brought up 23 times by 16 people, the following theme was created based on this code: "The Alice environment is useful in demonstrating most Java concepts, but cannot be used to demonstrate them all."

The following theme was based on the two most popular codes: "It is very easy to use" and "can be very fun and engaging." From an examination of the journal entries and student reactions in class, a strong case may be made that students have fun programming in Alice. Overall, the students were able to navigate the software easily. Only two students stated that they needed more resources for using the software.

The theme, "I am a beginner programmer and it is easier to make the connection to writing code when you can actually build it, manipulate it, and see it taking form in an animated environment," really ties in with the goal of the Alice environment. The following was taken directly from the Alice website (2013):

> Alice allows students to immediately see how their animation programs run, enabling them to easily understand the relationship between the programming statements and the behavior of objects in their animation. By manipulating the objects in their virtual world, students gain experience with all the programming constructs typically taught in an introductory programming course.

Some students had technical issues while using the Alice software and a few students found the Alice interface to be restricting. The two ideas were joined together by one student's comment that the research found to be representative of students that were frustrated: "I find it to be clunky and buggy, and while the basic idea to get users accustomed to object-oriented programming is good, it's just too much of a pain to implement complex movements or any sort of mathematical operation." The creators of the Alice software are using bug reporting to fix possible software issues in future versions. The software requires a sufficient amount of memory and a decent graphics card to run the three-dimensional graphics. Students have a variety of computers that they used for this course and not all of their computers run the software successfully. The software runs smoothly in the classrooms at the school, but many students choose to do their homework at home and not on the school provided computers.

Those students who thought that the software inappropriate for their level had prior programming experience. Since it is a Fundamentals of Programming course, it was unusual that 54% have had prior programming experience. As the students indicated however, this may be explained because fifty-seven percent of students registered for the course because it was required for their major. This compares with thirty-two percent who took it because they found the description of the course interesting, six percent take it to refresh their programming skills, and five percent take the course because it was recommended to them by an advisor or another student. It was clear that students that have extensive programming experience prefer to type the code instead of working with the Alice environment. This prompted the researcher to create the following theme: "I am not a fan of Alice. I have a lot of programming experience so I'd much rather dive right into the syntax."

The following theme was created based on journal entries that stated that Alice is good for one concept, but not for another: "The Alice environment is useful in demonstrating most Java concepts, but cannot be used to demonstrate them all". This theme came from a student's last journal entry summing up her thoughts about the previous journal entries. A few students commented on how Alice was not used as much in certain chapters, loops and arrays in particular. Some students recommended that more Alice activities be added to the course. The Alice exercise for arrays was beyond the scope of the course and was meant to challenge the students, but it could have impacted their perception of the usefulness of the Alice environment for teaching arrays. From the researcher's perspective, it is easier to develop Alice curriculum to teach classes, objects, methods, parameters, conditionals, and variables, than to develop curriculum to teach arithmetic, loops, and arrays. The lack of three-dimensional Alice models for the fall 2012, made it tough to create meaningful exercises; as more models are being added to the environment, it becomes easier to create curricular materials for the course.

Overall the tutors thought that the Alice environment was beneficial for teaching programming concepts. Many of them felt that Alice made programming exciting, allowed for creativity, and provided a visual representation of abstract concepts. A few of the tutors mentioned that the software was buggy at times and had some interface design issues. The tutors had an opportunity to work with students in the Fundamentals of Programming classes for at least two semesters; they worked with students in the treatment and control groups. Based on their experiences working with students, they felt that Alice was a valuable tool for teaching students how to program.

7.2   Research Questions and Answers

7.2.1   Control versus Treatment Group

This study questioned whether there were significant achievement and self-efficacy differences between students that learned object-oriented programming with Alice compared to students that learned in a traditional environment. The quantitative findings indicated that the treatment group had a higher mean for assignment scores, midterm scores, final scores, participation grades, course percentages, course grades, and growth for the following programming concepts: objects, classes, procedures, functions, conditionals, and programming overall. However, only the concept of procedures and the final exam scores were statistically significant.

Since the students with Alice performed at a higher rate on average for all achievement milestones than the students without Alice, it strengthens the case for using the Alice software.

94

The treatment group had a higher self-efficacy rate for procedures than the control group. The ability to program visual objects that you can see do an action (procedure) could increase self-efficacy. The final exam focused on conditionals, looping, classes, objects, arrays, and strings. Although Alice was not used as much for looping and arrays, the foundation of the Alice software centers on the idea of classes and objects. The user selects a class and then creates an object from that class; this is stressed from day one and so it does not seem unusual that the treatment group students would understand these concepts better on the final exam.

7.2.2   Demographics on Self-Efficacy, Success, and Perceptions

The last two research question answers were combined into one section to improve readability since both sections are based on demographic data. Demographics that did not have meaningful results were left out of this section. Quantitative as well as qualitative data were used to answer these questions. This study sought to determine whether demographics played a role in achievement and self-efficacy between the students using Alice and the students using the traditional environment and to determine the impact of demographic variables on student opinions of the Alice environment

7.2.2.1. Gender

Overall males started the semester having higher starting confidence level means for each programming concept. This is common since females typically rate their level of self-efficacy more conservatively (Beyer et al., 2005; Margolis & Fisher, 2002). When comparing females in the treatment group and control group, the treatment group had a statistically significant difference in confidence growth for the following areas: objects, classes, procedures, loops, and programming overall, with the following concepts approaching statistical significance: variables and conditionals. When comparing females in the treatment group and control group, the treatment group scored statistically significantly higher on their assignments, final exam, participation grade, overall percentages for the course, and overall course grades including withdrawals. Alice offers a different approach to teaching programming that may benefit women. West and Ross (2002) emphasize that formal mathematical teaching methods may not be appropriate for teaching females.

When asked to rate their perceptions of the Alice environment, females rated it statistically significantly higher than males for engagement, intuitiveness, and usefulness. Since there were fewer females compared to males, the qualitative data were normalized before making comparisons. Even though fifty-eight percent of technical difficulties were encounter by females, they had more positive attitudes about the environment (76%) and found it to be more cognitively beneficial (59%). They also appreciated the design of the environment (69%) more than males.

7.2.2.2. Age

The 22-29 year old students in the treatment group had statistically significantly higher scores than the control group on their assignments, their final exams, their participation points, and their percentage in the course. This age group can be referred to as digital natives and are known for being visual learners (Brumberger, 2011). Coates (2006) claims that this age group is the "most visual of all learning cohorts." Since Alice is visual, it lends itself well to this demographic.

7.2.2.3. Class Type (Afternoon, Evening, Online)

The online students found Alice to be statistically significantly more worthwhile for teaching looping and arrays; they also found Alice to be more intuitive, useful, and exciting than the face-to-face classes, but not statistically significant. Once the qualitative data were normalized, it was discovered that 77 percent of the students that found Alice to be engaging were online students.

Al-Bataineh, Brooks, and Bassoppo-Moyo (2005) recommended using visual aids when teaching online classes. The Alice environment can be thought of as a visual aid for representing programming concepts. The following quote was taken from an online student:

> As a "visual learner", I find the Alice environment to be not just helpful, but necessary to this course. I do not think I would be able to catch on as quickly on an online course if I didn't have some sort of visual representation to back up the language that is being taught.

7.2.2.4. Prior Programming Experience

The students with less prior programming experience found Alice to be statistically significantly more useful, engaging, and intuitive. Since the goal of the Alice software was to help teach students programming concepts in a more visual way, it makes sense that the experienced students that already had exposure to these concepts were not as intrigued and did not find it as beneficial.

The students without prior programming experience in the treatment group had statistically significantly higher assignment scores than the control group. The students had more assignments in the treatment group; this could be a detriment to the students as they are responsible for excess work or it could be helpful as they were required to complete more practice exercises.

There was no statistically significant difference between prior programming experience and success in the course. It is expected that students with prior programming experience would achieve at higher levels than those with no experience, but that was not supported by this study.

7.2.2.5. Major

The computer science majors in the treatment group had a statistically significantly higher level of growth than the control group for the following concepts: classes, procedures, functions, and programming overall. On average the computer science majors rated Alice higher than the other majors for its engagement, but this was not statistically significant.

After normalizing the qualitative data, the students in a computer science major had less general negative comments towards the Alice environment in their journal entries (20%). The math/engineering and students classified in the other category accounted for 82% of those that preferred typing code instead of using the drag and drop Alice environment. The math and engineering students seem to be content without having visualizations.

There were a fair amount of students who were considered experienced distributed across all three majors. Fifty-eight percent of the math and engineering majors were experienced, 48 percent of the computer science majors were experienced, and 47 percent of the other majors were experienced.

7.2.2.6. Semester

After normalizing the qualitative data, it was found that the spring 2012 semester had more technical issues (68%) than the fall 2012 semester (31%). The software was in beta during the spring 2012 semester and was released from beta before the fall 2012 semester. The spring 2012 and fall 2012 varied in perceived usefulness of the looping and arrays concepts. The Alice activities for the following concepts stayed the same except for a changing out the models (for example: old dancing tortoise versus new dancing tortoise): variables, procedures, functions, parameters, and conditionals. The looping and arrays exercises that were created for the spring 2012 semester had to be removed for the fall 2012 semester due to change of the three-dimensional models and reorganization of the environment; only one Alice exercise was created for looping and one for arrays. The fall 2012 array activity attempted was beyond the scope of the class; Alice models were sorted according to their height using a bubble sort (CS2 concept).

Students commented on the limitation of three-dimensional models in the environment; there were seven excerpts mentioning the lack of models. Five of the seven entries were from the fall 2012 semester. The Alice 3 software was in Beta in the spring 2012. The creators of Alice created new three-dimensional models for the fall 2012 release and they removed all of the old models. The new models were categorized into groups according to their skeletal makeup; this allowed programming of higher level classes. They started working on the models in the summer 2012, but there were limited models available for the fall 2012 semester. The beta version of the software that was used in the spring 2012 semester had hundreds of models that were created by CMU students assisting in the development of Alice. Since the beta release, the creators have gradually been adding new models to the environment.

7.3   Measure of Self-Efficacy

The regression analysis revealed that only 20% of the final course grade could be explained by self-efficacy; there are many other factors that contribute to success in the course. Some students filled out the journals more than once thinking that their entry did not submit; a few students adjusted their confidence levels from one submission to the next. Since confidence levels can change frequently, we cannot rely on them completely. Even though confidence can often change, we need to be aware of it since it can impact our motivation and interest in a subject area (Bandura 1996), which in turn impacts student retention in a course or a program (Militiadou and Savenye 2003).

7.4   Recommendations for Future Research

This study was only conducted over two semesters and the Alice software was still in beta for the spring 2012 semester. It would be interesting to repeat the study with two semesters with the software out of beta. The creators of the Alice software have been working to solve technical issues. Also, the software creators have continuously been adding new three dimensional models to the environment. Repeating this study in the future may help to reduce the number of students suffering from technical glitches in the software and the complaints of limited three-dimensional models. It would be interesting to see how this might impact students' perceptions of the software.

This study focused on the Alice environment, but there are many other visual tools for teaching programming concepts. This researcher did not find much research supporting the effectiveness of these other tools. It would be interesting to conduct this same study using a different tool for the treatment group. The Alice activities for this study were all animation based. Alice supports the ability to create interactive environments/games. It may be interesting to have the students create games to see if it increased male interest in the environment. Since this study had a strong impact on females, it may also be interesting to focus on how visual programming environments directly affect females at different age levels.

7.5   Conclusion

Overall, students found the Alice environment enjoyable, easy to use, and a great way to teach beginners programming concepts visually. On average, the courses using Alice achieved at a higher rate and had higher overall self-efficacy than the traditional courses. In response to the research question, females found Alice to be more engaging, intuitive, and useful than males; they had more general positive attitudes about the environment. Females in the Alice courses were also more successful and had more confidence in their abilities. Students majoring in a computer science tended to view Alice as more engaging. The computer science majors that used the Alice environment also had a higher growth in confidence for overall programming concepts. The students with less prior programming experience found Alice to be significantly more useful, engaging, and intuitive. The younger generation, digital natives, seem to academically benefit from the Alice environment. Online students seem to find the environment more captivating and receive the greatest benefit from using it.

Some students had trouble with software bugs, primarily because half of this study was conducted while the Alice software was still in a beta release; however, the software is continually improving. Although many of the students enjoyed using the Alice environment and found the drag and drop easy to use, some found it to be restricting. Some students mentioned that although the Alice environment is good for introducing programming concepts, it may not be good for all students.

This study helps support that Alice has the capability to raise performance rates and increase motivation towards programming (Cooper, Dan, & Pausch, 2003; Moskal, Lurie, & Cooper, 2004; Courte, Howard, & Bishop-Clark, 2006; Bishop-Clark, Courte, Evans, & Howard, 2007; Sykes, 2007; Johnsgard &McDonald, 2008; Daly, 2009; Mullins, Whitfield, & Conlon, 2009; Dann et al., 2012). This study used triangulation of methods to strengthen the results. The qualitative results were used to enrich and support the quantitative findings.

There have been many tools written over the past few decades to help students with learning how to program. "The theory of computing lends itself naturally to visualization techniques" (Cogliati et al., 2005, p. 1). Students have trouble processing abstract ideas (Cogliati et al., 2005; Fowler et al., 2000). Research shows that visual programming environments have the capability to improve comprehension of programming material, self-confidence levels, performance, retention rates, and motivation towards programming (Cooper, Dan, & Pausch, 2003; Moskal, Lurie, & Cooper, 2004; Courte, Howard, & Bishop-Clark, 2006; Bishop-Clark, Courte, Evans, & Howard, 2007; Dann et al. 2012; Johnsgard &McDonald, 2008; Mullins, Whitfield, & Conlon, 2009; Panitz, Sung, & Rosenberg, 2010; Daly, 2009; Sanders & Dorn, 2003 & 2004; Sykes, 2007; Vilner, Zur, & Tavor, 2011). The results of this study suggest that visual programming environments can enhance student learning.

APPENDIX A

INSTRUCTIONAL RESEARCH BOARD APPROVAL FOR STUDY

UNIVERSITY OF
NORTH·TEXAS

Discover the power of ideas.

September 13, 2011

Scott Warren
Department of Learning Technologies
University of North Texas

Re: Human Subjects Application No. 11379

Dear Dr. Warren:

As permitted by federal law and regulations governing the use of human subjects in research projects (45 CFR 46), the UNT Institutional Review Board has reviewed your proposed project titled "The Effects of Using Alice in a Fundamentals of Programming Course." The risks inherent in this research are minimal, and the potential benefits to the subject outweigh those risks. The submitted protocol is hereby approved for the use of human subjects in this study. **Federal Policy 45 CFR 46.109(e) stipulates that IRB approval is for one year only, September 13, 2011 to September 12, 2012.**

It is your responsibility according to U.S. Department of Health and Human Services regulations to submit annual and terminal progress reports to the IRB for this project. The IRB must also review this project prior to any modifications.

Please contact Shelia Bourns, Research Compliance Analyst, or Boyd Herndon, Director of Research Compliance, at extension 3940, if you wish to make changes or need additional information.

Sincerely,

Patricia L. Kaminski, Ph.D.
Associate Professor
Department of Psychology
Chair, Institutional Review Board

PK:sb

APPENDIX B

INFORMED CONSENT FOR GRANT PARTICIPATION

Study Title: Transition: Alice 2 to Alice 3 for Community Colleges

Principal Investigator: Wanda Dann, Director of Alice Project and Associate Teaching Professor
    [CS Department, 5000 Forbes Ave. Pittsburgh, PA, 15213, 412-268-9959, wpdann@cs.cmu.edu]

Other Investigator(s): Donald J. Slater, Assistant Teaching Professor, CMU, PA
    William Taylor, Associate Professor, Camden County College, NJ

Purpose of this Research and Evaluation

The purpose of the research and evaluation is to assess the effectiveness of an innovative approach for teaching fundamental programming concepts. The project uses a peer mentoring model and workshop materials designed to support community college faculty as they adopt the use of this innovative approach in their classrooms.

Procedures

At the beginning of the semester, you will be asked to complete a survey to tell us about your background in mathematics and computing, and your plans to take computer science courses.

At the beginning and again at the end of the semester, you will be asked to complete a survey containing questions about your perceptions about the course, computer science and your current plans to take computer science courses.

Participant Requirements

You are asked to participate in the research and evaluation because you will be enrolled in a computer science course at one of the community college sites.

Risks

The risks and discomfort associated with participation in this research and evaluation are no greater than those ordinarily encountered in daily life or during the performance of routine physical or psychological examinations or tests. No other risks are anticipated.

Benefits

Students are expected to experience a better comprehension of the fundamental concepts of computing as a result of the innovative use of ALICE. Participation in this research and evaluation allows students to impact the ways in which ALICE is and will be used by faculty.

Compensation & Costs

No compensation will be given to you as a participant in this research and evaluation. There will be no cost to you if you participate in this research and evaluation.

Confidentiality

By participating in the research and evaluation, you understand and agree that Carnegie Mellon may be required to disclose your consent form, data and other personally identifiable information as required by law, regulation, subpoena or court order. Otherwise, your confidentiality will be maintained in the following manner:

Your data and consent form will be kept separate. Your consent form will be stored in a locked location on Carnegie Mellon property and will not be disclosed to third parties. By participating, you understand and agree that the data and information gathered during this study may be used by Carnegie Mellon and published and/or disclosed by Carnegie Mellon to others outside of Carnegie Mellon. However, your name, address, contact information and other direct personal identifiers in your consent form or other data collection efforts will not be mentioned in any such publication or dissemination of the research data and/or results by Carnegie Mellon.

The researchers will take the following steps to protect participants' identities during this study: (1) Each participant will be assigned a number; (2) The researchers will record any data collected during the study by number, not by name; (3) Any original data files will be stored in a secured location accessed only by authorized researchers.

Rights

Your participation is voluntary. You are free to stop your participation at any point. Refusal to participate or withdrawal of your consent or discontinued participation in the study will not result in any penalty or loss of benefits or rights to which you might otherwise be entitled. The Principal Investigator may at his/her discretion remove you from the research and evaluation for any of a number of reasons. In such an event, you will not suffer any penalty or loss of benefits or rights which you might otherwise be entitled.

Right to Ask Questions & Contact Information

If you have any questions about this research and evaluation, desire additional information, or wish to withdraw your participation please contact the Principle Investigator by mail, phone or e-mail in accordance with the contact information listed on the first page of this consent.

If you have questions pertaining to your rights as a participant; or to report objections to this research and evaluation, you should contact the Research Regulatory Compliance Office at Carnegie Mellon University. Email: irb-review@andrew.cmu.edu . Phone: 412-268-1901 or 412-268-5460.

The Carnegie Mellon University Institutional Review Board (IRB) has approved the use of human participants for this study.

APPENDIX C

JOURNAL ENTRIES

Control Group	Treatment Group
Journal 1	Journal 1
Journal 2: Java Variables	Journal 2: Java and Alice Variables
Journal 3: Java Methods	Journal 3: Java and Alice Methods
Journal 4: Java Conditionals	Journal 4: Java and Alice Conditionals
Journal 5: Java Classes, Objects, and Loops	Journal 5: Java and Alice Classes, Objects, and Loops
Journal 6: Java Arrays	Journal 6: Java and Alice Arrays
Journal 7: Java – End of Course	Journal 7: Java and Alice – End of Course

Journal 1

* Required

What is your full name? *

What section of COSC1315 are you in enrolled in? *

- ○ S01
- ○ P01
- ○ S70
- ○ WW1
- ○ WW2
- ○ WW3

Ethnicity *

- ○ American Indian
- ○ African American
- ○ Asian
- ○ Caucasian
- ○ Hispanic
- ○ Multiracial
- ○ Other:

Gender *

○ Male

○ Female

Age *

○ Under 18

○ 18-21

○ 22-24

○ 25-29

○ 30-39

○ 40-49

○ 50 and up

Are you currently enrolled full-time (12 hours or more) or part-time (less than 12 hours)? *

○ Full-time

○ Part-time

How many college credits have you earned thus far? *

○ Less than 15

○ Between 15-30

○ Between 31 and 60

○ More than 60

What is your major? *

○ Computer Science

○ Web Programming

○ Computer Information Systems

○ Engineering

○ Gaming

○ Other: [_____]

Please mark the highest level to which you have studied each of the following items. *

	Have Not Studied	Self Taught	High School	College
Alice	○	○	○	○
Java	○	○	○	○
C	○	○	○	○
C++	○	○	○	○
Basic	○	○	○	○
Visual Basic	○	○	○	○
Pascal	○	○	○	○
Ada	○	○	○	○
Python	○	○	○	○
FORTRAN	○	○	○	○
HTML	○	○	○	○
Javascript	○	○	○	○
Other Scripting	○	○	○	○

Please rate your current understanding of the following programming concepts (5 being the highest level) *

	1	2	3	4	5
variables	○	○	○	○	○
objects	○	○	○	○	○
classes	○	○	○	○	○
procedures	○	○	○	○	○
functions	○	○	○	○	○
methods overall	○	○	○	○	○
parameters	○	○	○	○	○
conditionals	○	○	○	○	○
loops	○	○	○	○	○
arrays	○	○	○	○	○
programming overall	○	○	○	○	○

111

What is your reason for taking this course? *

- ○ Required for major
- ○ Recommended by advisor
- ○ Heard about it in COSC1301/BCIS1305 and thought it might be interesting
- ○ Read about it in the catalog and was interested in learning more about programming
- ○ This is my second time taking the course
- ○ I have programming experience and thought that this would be an easy A
- ○ Other: [   ]

If you are taking this class as an online course, what is the reason? Please skip this question if you are not taking this course online.

- ○ Class times didn't fit with work schedule
- ○ Have young children and need to be home with them
- ○ Didn't have time for face-to-face class
- ○ I live far away
- ○ English as second language
- ○ Other: [   ]

[Submit]

Powered by Google Docs

Journal 2 - Java Variables

* Required

What is your full name? *

[   ]

What section of COSC1315 are you in enrolled in? *

○ P01

○ S70

○ WW2

What activity/activities were the most challenging in chapters 1-3? Why? *

[   ]

What activity/activities were the most enjoyable in chapters 1-3? Why? *

[   ]

Explain how variables are useful in your own words. *

[   ]

How well have you been able to manage your time? *

```



```

Which of the following helped you to complete the class exercises? Check all that apply. *

☐ Attending class

☐ Watching the chapter (Wimba) videos

☐ Reading through the class exercises

☐ I didn't do the class exercises

The chapter (Wimba) videos helped me to understand the material. Please skip this question if you didn't watch any of the videos.

	1	2	3	4	5	
Strongly Disagree	◯	◯	◯	◯	◯	Strongly Agree

Please rate your current understanding of "variables". *

	1	2	3	4	5	
Low	◯	◯	◯	◯	◯	High

Please rate your current comfort level of using variables in Java code. *

	1	2	3	4	5	
Low	◯	◯	◯	◯	◯	High

[Submit]

Powered by Google Docs

Journal 2 - Java and Alice Variables

* Required

What is your full name? *

[   ]

What section of COSC1315 are you in enrolled in? *

○ S01

○ P70

○ WW1

What activity/activities were the most challenging in chapters 1-3? Why? *

[   ]

What activity/activities were the most enjoyable in chapters 1-3? Why? *

Explain how variables are useful in your own words. *

How well have you been able to manage your time? *

Which of the following helped you to complete the class exercises? Check all that apply. *

☐ Attending class

☐ Watching the chapter (Wimba) videos

☐ Reading through the class exercises

☐ I didn't do the class exercises

The chapter (Wimba) videos helped me to understand the material. Please skip this question if you didn't watch any of the videos.

          1   2   3   4   5

Strongly Disagree ○ ○ ○ ○ ○ Strongly Agree

Please rate your current understanding of "variables". *

     1   2   3   4   5

Low ○ ○ ○ ○ ○ High

Please rate your current comfort level of using variables in Java code. *

     1   2   3   4   5

Low ○ ○ ○ ○ ○ High

Alice helped me understand "variables". *

          1   2   3   4   5

Strongly Disagree ○ ○ ○ ○ ○ Strongly Agree

I found Alice engaging (e.g., the software kept my attention). *

          1   2   3   4   5

Strongly Disagree ○ ○ ○ ○ ○ Strongly Agree

I found Alice easy to use. *

          1   2   3   4   5

Strongly Disagree ○ ○ ○ ○ ○ Strongly Agree

How do you feel about the Alice environment? *

[text box]

Submit

Journal 3 - Java Methods

* Required

What is your full name? *

[text field]

What section of COSC1315 are you in enrolled in? *

○ P01

○ S70

○ WW2

What activity/activities were the most challenging in chapters 4-5? Why? *

[text box]

What activity/activities were the most enjoyable in chapters 4-5? Why? *

Explain how methods are useful in your own words. *

How well have you been able to manage your time? *

Which of the following helped you to complete the class exercises? Check all that apply. *

☐ Attending class

☐ Watching the chapter (Wimba) videos

☐ Reading through the class exercises

☐ I didn't do the class exercises

The chapter (Wimba) videos helped me to understand the material. Please skip this question if you didn't watch any of the videos.

              1   2   3   4   5

Strongly Disagree ○   ○   ○   ○   ○ Strongly Agree

Please rate your current understanding of "procedures". *

      1   2   3   4   5

Low ○   ○   ○   ○   ○ High

Please rate your current comfort level of using procedures in Java code. *

      1   2   3   4   5

Low ○   ○   ○   ○   ○ High

Please rate your current understanding of "functions". *

      1   2   3   4   5

Low ○   ○   ○   ○   ○ High

Please rate your current comfort level of using functions in Java code. *

      1   2   3   4   5

Low ○   ○   ○   ○   ○ High

Please rate your current understanding of methods overall. *

      1   2   3   4   5

Low ○   ○   ○   ○   ○ High

Please rate your current comfort level of using methods in Java code. *

      1   2   3   4   5

Low ○   ○   ○   ○   ○ High

Submit

Journal 3 - Java and Alice Methods

* Required

What is your full name? *

[   ]

What section of COSC1315 are you in enrolled in? *

○ S01

○ P70

○ WW1

What activity/activities were the most challenging in chapters 4-5? Why? *

[   ]

What activity/activities were the most enjoyable in chapters 4-5? Why? *

Explain how methods are useful in your own words. *

How well have you been able to manage your time? *

Which of the following helped you to complete the class exercises? Check all that apply. *

☐ Attending class

☐ Watching the chapter (Wimba) videos

☐ Reading through the class exercises

☐ I didn't do the class exercises

The chapter (Wimba) videos helped me to understand the material. Please skip this question if you didn't watch any of the videos.

        1   2   3   4   5

Strongly Disagree ⊙ ⊙ ⊙ ⊙ ⊙ Strongly Agree

Please rate your current understanding of "procedures". *

  1   2   3   4   5

Low ○ ○ ○ ○ ○ High

Please rate your current comfort level of using procedures in Java code. *

  1   2   3   4   5

Low ○ ○ ○ ○ ○ High

Alice helped me understand "procedures". *

  1   2   3   4   5

Strongly Disagree ○ ○ ○ ○ ○ Strongly Agree

Please rate your current understanding of "functions". *

  1   2   3   4   5

Low ○ ○ ○ ○ ○ High

Please rate your current comfort level of using functions in Java code. *

  1   2   3   4   5

Low ○ ○ ○ ○ ○ High

Alice helped me understand "functions". *

  1   2   3   4   5

Strongly Disagree ○ ○ ○ ○ ○ Strongly Agree

Please rate your current understanding of methods overall. *

  1   2   3   4   5

Low ○ ○ ○ ○ ○ High

Please rate your current comfort level of using methods in Java code. *

  1   2   3   4   5

Low ○ ○ ○ ○ ○ High

Alice helped me understand methods. *

  1   2   3   4   5

Strongly Disagree ○ ○ ○ ○ ○ Strongly Agree

I found Alice engaging (e.g., the software kept my attention). *

	1	2	3	4	5	
Strongly Disagree	○	○	○	○	○	Strongly Agree

I found Alice easy to use. *

	1	2	3	4	5	
Strongly Disagree	○	○	○	○	○	Strongly Agree

How do you feel about the Alice environment? *

[text box]

[Submit]

Powered by Google Docs

Journal 4 - Java Conditionals

* Required
What is your full name? *

[text field]

What section of COSC1315 are you in enrolled in? *

○ P01

○ S70

○ WW2

What activity/activities were the most challenging in chapter 6? Why? *

[text box]

What activity/activities were the most enjoyable in chapter 6? Why? *

Explain how conditionals are useful in your own words. *

How well have you been able to manage your time? *

Which of the following helped you to complete the class exercises? Check all that apply. *

☐ Attending class

☐ Watching the chapter (Wimba) videos

☐ Reading through the class exercises

☐ I didn't do the class exercises

The chapter (Wimba) videos helped me to understand the material. Please skip this question if you didn't watch any of the videos.

　　　　　　　　　1　2　3　4　5

Strongly Disagree ⊙ ⊙ ⊙ ⊙ ⊙ Strongly Agree

Please rate your current understanding of conditionals. *

　　1　2　3　4　5

Low ⊙ ⊙ ⊙ ⊙ ⊙ High

Please rate your current comfort level of using conditionals in Java code. *

　　1　2　3　4　5

Low ⊙ ⊙ ⊙ ⊙ ⊙ High

[Submit]

Powered by Google Docs

Journal 4 - Java and Alice Conditionals

* Required
What is your full name? *

```
[                    ]
```

What section of COSC1315 are you in enrolled in? *

○ S01

○ P70

○ WW1

What activity/activities were the most challenging in chapter 6? Why? *

```
[                                                        ]
[                                                        ]
[                                                        ]
[                                                        ]
[                                                        ]
[                                                        ]
```

What activity/activities were the most enjoyable in chapter 6? Why? *

Explain how conditionals are useful in your own words. *

How well have you been able to manage your time? *

Which of the following helped you to complete the class exercises? Check all that apply. *

☐ Attending class

☐ Watching the chapter (Wimba) videos

☐ Reading through the class exercises

☐ I didn't do the class exercises

The chapter (Wimba) videos helped me to understand the material. Please skip this question if you didn't watch any of the videos.

         1   2   3   4   5

Strongly Disagree ⊙ ⊙ ⊙ ⊙ ⊙ Strongly Agree

Please rate your current understanding of conditionals. *

      1   2   3   4   5

Low ⊙ ⊙ ⊙ ⊙ ⊙ High

Please rate your current comfort level of using conditionals in Java code. *

      1   2   3   4   5

Low ⊙ ⊙ ⊙ ⊙ ⊙ High

Alice helped me understand conditionals. *

	1	2	3	4	5	
Strongly Disagree	○	○	○	○	○	Strongly Agree

I found Alice engaging (e.g., the software kept my attention). *

	1	2	3	4	5	
Strongly Disagree	○	○	○	○	○	Strongly Agree

I found Alice easy to use. *

	1	2	3	4	5	
Strongly Disagree	○	○	○	○	○	Strongly Agree

How do you feel about the Alice environment? *

Submit

Journal 5 - Java Classes, Objects, and Loops

* Required

What is your full name? *

[   ]

What section of COSC1315 are you in enrolled in? *

- ⊙ P01
- ⊙ S70
- ⊙ WW2

What activity/activities were the most challenging in chapters 7-9? Why? *

[   ]

What activity/activities were the most enjoyable in chapters 7-9? Why? *

[   ]

What activity/activities were the most challenging in chapter 10? Why? *

[   ]

What activity/activities were the most enjoyable in chapter 10? Why? *

Explain how loops are useful in your own words. *

How well have you been able to manage your time? *

Which of the following helped you to complete the class exercises? Check all that apply. *

☐ Attending class

☐ Watching the chapter (Wimba) videos

☐ Reading through the class exercises

☐ I didn't do the class exercises

The chapter (Wimba) videos helped me to understand the material. Please skip this question if you didn't watch any of the videos.

         1   2   3   4   5

Strongly Disagree   ○   ○   ○   ○   ○   Strongly Agree

Please rate your current understanding of loops. *

     1   2   3   4   5

Low   ○   ○   ○   ○   ○   High

Please rate your current comfort level of using loops in Java code. *

     1   2   3   4   5

Low   ○   ○   ○   ○   ○   High

Please rate your current understanding of classes and objects. *

     1   2   3   4   5

Low   ○   ○   ○   ○   ○   High

Please rate your current comfort level of using classes and objects in Java code. *

     1   2   3   4   5

Low   ○   ○   ○   ○   ○   High

[Submit]

Powered by Google Docs

Journal 5 - Java and Alice Classes, Objects, and Loops

* Required

What is your full name? *

What section of COSC1315 are you in enrolled in? *

- ○ S01
- ○ P70
- ○ WW1

What activity/activities were the most challenging in chapters 7-9? Why? *

What activity/activities were the most enjoyable in chapters 7-9? Why? *

What activity/activities were the most challenging in chapter 10? Why? *

What activity/activities were the most enjoyable in chapter 10? Why? *

Explain how loops are useful in your own words. *

How well have you been able to manage your time? *

Which of the following helped you to complete the class exercises? Check all that apply. *

- ☐ Attending class
- ☐ Watching the chapter (Wimba) videos
- ☐ Reading through the class exercises
- ☐ I didn't do the class exercises

The chapter (Wimba) videos helped me to understand the material. Please skip this question if you didn't watch any of the videos.

	1	2	3	4	5	
Strongly Disagree	○	○	○	○	○	Strongly Agree

Please rate your current understanding of loops. *

    1   2   3   4   5

Low ○ ○ ○ ○ ○ High

Please rate your current comfort level of using loops in Java code. *

    1   2   3   4   5

Low ○ ○ ○ ○ ○ High

Alice helped me understand loops. *

        1   2   3   4   5

Strongly Disagree ○ ○ ○ ○ ○ Strongly Agree

Please rate your current understanding of classes and objects. *

    1   2   3   4   5

Low ○ ○ ○ ○ ○ High

Please rate your current comfort level of using classes and objects in Java code. *

    1   2   3   4   5

Low ○ ○ ○ ○ ○ High

Alice helped me to understand classes and objects. *

        1   2   3   4   5

Strongly Disagree ○ ○ ○ ○ ○ Strongly Agree

I found Alice engaging (e.g., the software kept my attention). *

    1   2   3   4   5

Strongly Disagree ⊙ ⊙ ⊙ ⊙ ⊙ Strongly Agree

I found Alice easy to use. *

    1   2   3   4   5

Strongly Disagree ⊙ ⊙ ⊙ ⊙ ⊙ Strongly Agree

How do you feel about the Alice environment? *

Submit

Powered by Google Docs

Journal 6 - Java Arrays

* Required
What is your full name? *

What section of COSC1315 are you in enrolled in? *

⊙ P01

⊙ S70

⊙ WW2

What activity/activities were the most challenging in chapter 11? Why? *

What activity/activities were the most enjoyable in chapter 11? Why? *

Explain how arrays are useful in your own words. *

How well have you been able to manage your time? *

Which of the following helped you to complete the class exercises? Check all that apply. *

☐ Attending class

☐ Watching the chapter (Wimba) videos

☐ Reading through the class exercises

☐ I didn't do the class exercises

The chapter (Wimba) videos helped me to understand the material. Please skip this question if you didn't watch any of the videos.

       1 2 3 4 5

Strongly Disagree ◎ ◎ ◎ ◎ ◎ Strongly Agree

Please rate your current understanding of arrays. *

    1   2   3   4   5

Low ○ ○ ○ ○ ○ High

Please rate your current comfort level of using arrays in Java code. *

    1   2   3   4   5

Low ○ ○ ○ ○ ○ High

[Submit]

Powered by Google Docs

Journal 6 - Java and Alice Arrays

* Required

What is your full name? *

[   ]

What section of COSC1315 are you in enrolled in? *

○ S01

○ P70

○ WW1

What activity/activities were the most challenging in chapter 11? Why? *

[   ]

139

What activity/activities were the most enjoyable in chapter 11? Why? *

Explain how arrays are useful in your own words. *

How well have you been able to manage your time? *

Which of the following helped you to complete the class exercises? Check all that apply. *

☐ Attending class

☐ Watching the chapter (Wimba) videos

☐ Reading through the class exercises

☐ I didn't do the class exercises

The chapter (Wimba) videos helped me to understand the material. Please skip this question if you didn't watch any of the videos.

          1   2   3   4   5

Strongly Disagree ◯ ◯ ◯ ◯ ◯ Strongly Agree

Please rate your current understanding of arrays. *

1 2 3 4 5

Low ⊙ ⊙ ⊙ ⊙ ⊙ High

Please rate your current comfort level of using arrays in Java code. *

1 2 3 4 5

Low ⊙ ⊙ ⊙ ⊙ ⊙ High

Alice helped me understand arrays. *

1 2 3 4 5

Strongly Disagree ⊙ ⊙ ⊙ ⊙ ⊙ Strongly Agree

I found Alice engaging (e.g., the software kept my attention). *

1 2 3 4 5

Strongly Disagree ⊙ ⊙ ⊙ ⊙ ⊙ Strongly Agree

I found Alice easy to use. *

1 2 3 4 5

Strongly Disagree ⊙ ⊙ ⊙ ⊙ ⊙ Strongly Agree

How do you feel about the Alice environment? *

[Submit]

Powered by Google Docs

141

Journal 7 - Java - End of Course

* Required
What is your full name? *

[   ]

What section of COSC1315 are you in enrolled in? *

- ○ S70
- ○ P01
- ○ WW2

Please rate your current understanding of the following programming concepts (5 being the highest level) *

	1	2	3	4	5
variables	○	○	○	○	○
objects	○	○	○	○	○
classes	○	○	○	○	○
procedures	○	○	○	○	○
functions	○	○	○	○	○
methods overall	○	○	○	○	○
parameters	○	○	○	○	○
conditionals	○	○	○	○	○
loops	○	○	○	○	○
arrays	○	○	○	○	○
programming overall	○	○	○	○	○

I watched the Wimba videos: *

Never ▾

The chapter (Wimba) videos helped me to understand the material. Please skip this question if you didn't watch any of the videos.

	1	2	3	4	5	
Strongly Disagree	○	○	○	○	○	Strongly Agree

How well have you been able to manage your time throughout the course? *

What activity/activities were the most challenging in the course? *

What activity/activities were the most enjoyable in the course? *

143

Are you going to take another programming course? If so, what course? *

What is your major? Did this course effect your decision in any way? *

Do you have any ideas for of anything that could be added to the course? *

Submit

Journal 7 - Java and Alice - End of Course

* Required
What is your full name? *

What section of COSC1315 are you in enrolled in? *

- ○ P70
- ○ S01
- ○ WW1

Please rate your current understanding of the following programming concepts (5 being the highest level) *

	1	2	3	4	5
variables	○	○	○	○	○
objects	○	○	○	○	○
classes	○	○	○	○	○
procedures	○	○	○	○	○
functions	○	○	○	○	○
methods overall	○	○	○	○	○
parameters	○	○	○	○	○
conditionals	○	○	○	○	○
loops	○	○	○	○	○
arrays	○	○	○	○	○
programming overall	○	○	○	○	○

Please rate the degree to which Alice helped you to understand the following programming concepts (5 being the highest level) *

	1	2	3	4	5
variables	○	○	○	○	○
objects	○	○	○	○	○
classes	○	○	○	○	○
procedures	○	○	○	○	○
functions	○	○	○	○	○
methods overall	○	○	○	○	○
parameters	○	○	○	○	○
conditionals	○	○	○	○	○
loops	○	○	○	○	○
arrays	○	○	○	○	○

Alice helped me to understand computer programming concepts *

         1   2   3   4   5

Strongly Disagree ◎ ◎ ◎ ◎ ◎ Strongly Agree

I found Alice engaging (e.g., the software kept my attention). *

         1   2   3   4   5

Strongly Disagree ◎ ◎ ◎ ◎ ◎ Strongly Agree

I found Alice easy to use. *

         1   2   3   4   5

Strongly Disagree ◎ ◎ ◎ ◎ ◎ Strongly Agree

How do you feel about the Alice environment? *

I watched the Wimba videos: *

Never	▼

The chapter (Wimba) videos helped me to understand the material. Please skip this question if you didn't watch any of the videos.

         1   2   3   4   5

Strongly Disagree ◎ ◎ ◎ ◎ ◎ Strongly Agree

How well have you been able to manage your time throughout the course? *

What activity/activities were the most challenging in the course? *

What activity/activities were the most enjoyable in the course? *

Are you going to take another programming course? If so, what course? *

What is your major? Did this course effect your decision in any way? *

Do you have any ideas for of anything that could be added to the course? *

Submit

Powered by Google Docs

APPENDIX D

CHAPTER OBJECTIVES

Chapter 1

- ☑ Explain the difference between high and low level programming languages
- ☑ Describe the history of how the Java programming language was started.
- ☑ Briefly describe the following:
    - ○ Object Oriented Programming
    - ○ Platform-Independence
    - ○ Garbage Collection
    - ○ Java Developer's Kit
- ☑ Explain the difference between Java applets, applications, and servlets
- ☑ Explain the difference between Java and JavaScript
- ☑ Compile and execute a Java program
- ☑ Debug errors
- ☑ Identify and fix compiler errors

Chapter 2

- ☑ Describe the term variable.
- ☑ Create valid variable names by following Java's syntactical and stylistic rules.
- ☑ Name and describe each of the primitive types used in the Java language.
- ☑ Declare and assign values to variables.
- ☑ Use comments, strings, and statements properly in coding.
- ☑ Describe String concatenation.
- ☑ Use escape codes to format output.
- ☑ List the rules of precedence in order.
- ☑ Apply precedence rules to solve arithmetic Java statements.
- ☑ Solve arithmetic Java statements that include a mixture of the 5 arithmetic operators.
- ☑ Match shorthand assignment operators with their equivalent longhand notations.
- ☑ Apply casting rules to coding situations.

Chapter 3

- ☑ Apply formats (currency and percentages) to output.
- ☑ Use keyboard input in Java program to create interactivity.
- ☑ Use dialog box input/output in Java program to create interactivity.
- ☑ Associate import statements with corresponding input/output/format classes/packages.

Chapter 4

- ☑ Properly construct and use methods when programming.
- ☑ Build methods with:
    - ○ No Arguments and No Return Values
    - ○ Some Arguments and No Return Values
- ☑ Use arguments and return values properly.
- ☑ Create a library and call methods from the library from another class.
- ☑ Explain the purpose of the Java API.

Chapter 5

☑ Properly construct and use methods when programming.
☑ Describe the difference between a procedural method and a functional method.
☑ Use the Java Application Interface to code programs.
☑ Place methods into a separate file and call them from main program.

Chapter 6

☑ List relational operators.
☑ List logical operators.
☑ Use the hierarchy of operators chart to properly construct if/else statements.
☑ Construct switch statements.
☑ Use nested if statements.

Chapter 7

☑ Explain encapsulation, inheritance, and polymorphism.
☑ Create and explain the use of constructors.
☑ Locate Java source files.
☑ Use accessor and mutator methods.
☑ Create a program that inherits properties from another program.
☑ Create a package for a group of programs.
☑ Explain the difference between the IDE and JDK.
☑ Write programs without the Java IDE.

Chapter 8

☑ Create JFrames that hold a container called a contentPane.
☑ Use Layouts for setting up GUI elements.
☑ Create JPanels for adding components.
☑ Form components:
   o JLabel
   o JButton
   o JTextField
☑ Graphic components:
   o Strings
   o Images
   o Lines
   o Rectangles
   o Ovals
   o Polygons
   o Arcs
☑ Change the color and font of elements.

Chapter 9

☑ Use listeners and event handling methods.

Chapter 10

☑ Code programs using the following looping techniques:
   - While Loop
   - Do While Loop
   - For Loop
☑ Explain when the Break and Continue statements would be used when coding loops.
☑ Walk through While, Do While, and For loops documenting variables as they change.

Chapter 11

☑ Declare and use arrays in programs.
☑ Access array elements within an array.
☑ Calculate the sum, largest number, smallest number, and average of a group of numbers by using an array.
☑ Setup a program to store the arguments from command line into an array.

Chapter 12

☑ Explain String concatenation.
☑ Use the StringTokenizer to determine the total number of words typed by the user.
☑ Use the following String methods:
   - length()
   - charAt()
   - substring()
   - indexOf()
   - toUpperCase()
   - toLowerCase()
   - startsWith()
   - endsWith()
   - compareTo()
   - replace()
   - trim()
   - equals()
   - equalsIgnoreCase()

REFERENCES

Alice Website. (n.d.). Retrieved February 21, 2013, from http://www.alice.org/

Al-Bataineh, A., Brooks, S. L., & Bassoppo-Moyo, T. C. (2005). Implications of online teaching and learning. *International Journal of Instructional Media, 32*, 285.

Al-Linjawi, A. & Al-Nuaim, H. (2010) Using Alice to teach novice programmers OOP concepts. *JKAU: Sci., 22*, 59-68.

App Inventor Website. (n.d.). Retrieved June 17, 2012, from http://www.appinventor.mit.edu/

Ashcraft, C. & Blithe, S. (2009). *Women in IT: The facts.* Retrieved from http://www.ncwit.org/pdf/NCWIT_TheFacts_rev2010.pdf

Baltie Website. (n.d.). Retrieved July 16, 2012, from http://www.sgpsys.com/en/

Bandura, A. (1993). Perceived self-efficacy in cognitive development and functioning. *Educational Psychology, 28*, 117–148.

Bandura, A., Barbaranelli, C., Caprara, G., & Pastorelli, C. (1996). Multifaceted impact of self-efficacy beliefs on academic functioning. *Child Development, 67*, 1206–1222.

Ben-Ari, M. (1998). Constructivism in computer science. Proceedings from SIGCSE '98: *The 29th SIGCSE Technical Symposium on Computer Science Education.* (pp. 257-261). New York, NY: Association for Computing Machinery.

Beyer, S. DeKeuster, M., Walter, K., Colar, M. & Holcomb, C. (2005). Changes in CS students' attitudes towards CS over time: An examination of gender differences. Proceedings from SIGCSE '05: *The 36th SIGCSE Technical Symposium on Computer Science Education.* (pp. 392-396). New York, NY: Association for Computing Machinery.

Bishop-Clark, C., Courte, J., Evans, D., & Howard, E. (2007). A quantitative and qualitative investigation of using Alice programming to improve confidence, enjoyment, and achievement among non-majors. *Journal of Educational Computing Research, 37*, 193-207.

Bonar, J. & Soloway, E. (1983). Uncovering principles of novice programming. Proceedings from POPL '83: *The 10th ACM SIGACT-SIGPLAN Symposium on Principles of Programming Languages.* (pp. 10-13). New York, NY: Association for Computing Machinery.

Brumberger, E. (2011). Visual literacy and the digital native: An examination of the millennial learner. *Journal of Visual Literacy, 30*, 19-46.

Carlisle, M. C., Wilson, T. A., Humphries, J. W., & Hadfield, S. M. (2005). RAPTOR: A visual programming environment for teaching algorithmic problem solving. Proceedings from

SIGCSE '05: *The 36th SIGCSE Technical Symposium on Computer Science Education.* (pp. 176-180). New York, NY: Association for Computing Machinery.

Cliburn, D. (2008). Student opinions of Alice in CS1. Proceeding from FIE '08: *The 38th Annual Frontiers in Education Conference.* (pp. 1-6). Saratoga Springs, NY: IEEE Xplore.

Coates, J. (2006). *Generational learning styles.* River Falls, WI: LERN Books.

Cogliati, J., Goosey, F., Grinder, M., Pascoe, B., Ross, R., Williams, C. (2005). Realizing the promise of visualization in the theory of computing. *Journal on Educational Resource in Computing, 5,* 1-17.

Cohen, Jacob (1992). Statistics a power primer. *Psychology Bulletin, 112,* 155–159.

Cooper, S., Dann, W., & Pausch, R. (2003). Teaching objects-first in introductory computer science. Proceedings from SIGCSE '03: *The 34th SIGCSE Technical Symposium on Computer Science Education.* (pp. 191-195). New York, NY: Association for Computing Machinery.

Courte, J., Howard, E., & Bishop-Clark, C. (2006). Using Alice in a computer science survey course. *Information Systems Education Journal, 4,* 1-7.

Daly, T. (2009, Fall). Using introductory programming tools to teach programming concepts: A literature review. *Journal for Computing Teachers.* 1-6.

Daly, T. (2010). Determining computer programming traits. *Journal of Computing Sciences in Colleges, 4,* 1.

Dann, W., Cosgrove, D., Slater, D., Culyba, D., & Cooper, S. (2012). Mediated transfer: Alice 3 to Java. Proceedings from SIGCSE '12: *The 43rd ACM technical symposium on Computer Science Education.* (pp. 141-146). New York, NY: Association for Computing Machinery.

Dann, W., Cooper, S., & Pausch, R. (2007). *Learning to program with Alice.* Upper Saddle River, NJ: Prentice Hall. Australia.

De Palma, P. (2001). Why women avoid computer science, *Communications of the ACM, 44,* 27-29.

Dingle, A., & Zander, C. (2001). Assessing the ripple effect of CS1 language choice, *J. Comput. Small Coll., 16,* 85–93.

Finlay, L. (2002). "Outing" the researcher: The provenance, process, and practice of reflexivity. *Qualitative Health Research, 12,* 531-545.

Fowler, L., Allen, M., Armarego, J., & Mackenzie, J. (2000). Learning styles and CASE tools in software engineering. *The 9th Annual Teaching Learning Forum.* (pp. 1-10). Perth, W.A.: Murdoch University Library.

GameMaker Website. Retrieved October 2009, from http://www.yoyogames.com

Garlick, R. & Cankaya, E. (2010). Using Alice in CS1: A quantitative experiment. Proceedings from ITiCSE '10: *The fifteenth annual conference on Innovation and technology in computer science education.* (pp. 165-168). Washington, DC: Association for Computing Machinery.

George, D., & Mallery, P. (2003). *SPSS for Windows step by step: A simple guide and reference.* 11.0 update (4th ed.). Boston, MA: Allyn & Bacon.

Greenfoot Website. (n.d.). Retrieved September 1, 2012, from http://www.greenfoot.org

Hadjerrouit. S. (1999). A constructivist approach to object-oriented design and programming. *SIGCSE Bulletin, 31*, 171-174.

Huck, S. (2004). *Reading statistics and research.* Boston, MA: Pearson Education.

Hundhausen, C. (1999). *Toward effective algorithm visualization artifacts: Designing for participation and communication in an undergraduate algorithms course.* Dissertation, Washington State University, Pullman, Washington.

Jeroo Website. (n.d.). Retrieved October 14, 2011, from http://www.jeroo.org

Johnsgard, K., & McDonald, J. (2008). Using ALICE in overview courses to improve success rates in programming I. Proceedings from CSEET '08: *The 21st Conference on Software Engineering Education and Training.* (pp. 129-136). Washington, DC: Association for Computing Machinery.

Kanuka, H. and Anderson, T. (1999). Using constructivism in technology-mediated learning: constructing order out of the chaos in the literature. *Radical Pedagogy.* Retrieved from: http://radicalpedagogy.icaap.org/content/issue1_2/02kanuka1_2.html

Kvale, S. (1996). InterViews : An introduction to qualitative research interviewing. *Sage Publications*, 241-242.

Lahtinen, E., Ala-Mutka, K., & Järvinen, H. (2005). A study of the difficulties of novice programmers. Proceedings from ITiCSE '05: *The 10th Annual SIGCSE Conference on innovation and Technology in Computer Science Education.* (pp. 14-18). New York, NY: Association for Computing Machinery.

Lanttazi, M.R. & Henry, S.M. (1996). Teaching the object-oriented paradigm and software reuse: notes from an empirical study. *Computer Science Education, 7*, 99-108.

MacKinnon, S. (2002). Technology integration in the classroom: Is there only one way to make it effective? *TechKnowLogia: International Journal of Technologies for the Advancement of Knowledge and Learning,* 57-60.

Malan, D. J., & Leitner, H. H. (2007). Scratch for budding computer scientists. *SIGCSE Bulletin. 39*, 223-227.

Margolis, J., & Fisher, A. (2002). Unlocking the clubhouse: Women in computing. *MIT Press*. 1-15.

Mauer, T.J. & Andrews K.D. (2000). Traditional, Likert, and simplified measures of self-efficacy. *Educational and Psychological Measurement, 60,* 970-973.

Maurer, T. J., & Pierce, H. R. (1998). A comparison of Likert scale and traditional measures of self-efficacy. *Journal of Applied Psychology, 83,* 324-329.

Militiadou, M., & Savenye, W. (2003). Applying social cognitive constructs of motivation to enhance student success in online distance education. *AACE Journal, 11,* 78-95.

Moskal, B., Lurie, D., & Cooper, S. (2004). Evaluating the effectiveness of a new instructional approach. *SIGCSE Bulletin, 36,* 75-79.

Mow, C. (2008). Issues and difficulties in teaching novice computer programming. *Innovative Techniques in Instruction Technology, E-learning, E-assessment, and Education,* Netherlands, 199-204.

Mullins, P., Whitfield, D., & Conlon, M. (2009). Using Alice 2.0 as a first language. *Journal of Computing Sciences in Colleges, 24,* 136-143.

Naps, T., Rößling, G., Almstrum, V., Dann, W., Fleischer, R., Hundhausen, C., Korhonen, A., Malmi, L., McNally, M., Rodger, S., & Velázquez-Iturbide, J. (2002). Exploring the role of visualization and engagement in computer science education. Proceedings from ITiCSE-WGR '02: *Working group reports from ITiCSE on Innovation and technology in computer science education.* (pp. 131-152). New York, NY: Association for Computing Machinery.

Panitz, M., Sung, K., & Rosenberg, R. (2010). Game programming in CS0: A scaffolded approach. *J. Comput. Small Coll, 26,* 126-132.

Perkins, D.N. (1991). Technology meets constructivism: Do they make a marriage? *Educational Technology, 31,* 18-23.

Petre, M. (2007). *Computer science education research.* New York, NY: Taylor & Francis.

Phye, G.D. (1997). *Handbook of academic learning: Construction of knowledge.* London: Academic Press.

Powers, K., Gross, P., Cooper, S., McNally, M., Goldman, K. J., & Proulx, V. (2006). Tools for teaching introductory programming: what works? Proceedings from SIGCSE '06: *The 37th SIGCSE Technical Symposium on Computer Science Education.* (pp. 560-561). New York, NY: Association for Computing Machinery.

Polya, G . (1948). *How to solve it: A new aspect of mathematical method*. Princeton, NJ : Princeton University Press.

Robins, A., Roundtree, J., & Roundtree, N. (2003). Learning and teaching programming: A review and discussion. *Computer Science Education, 13*, 137-172.

Robson, C. (2002). *Real world research: A resources for social scientists and practitioner-researchers*. Malden, MA: Blackwell Publishing Limited.

Sanders, D., & Dorn, B. (2003). Classroom experience with Jeroo. *Journal of Computing Sciences in Colleges, 18*, 308-316.

Sanders, D. & Dorn, B. (2004). Object-oriented programming with Jeroo in the information technology classroom. Proceedings from ISECON '04. (pp. 1-10). Newport, RI: EDSIG.

Schulte, C. & Bennedsen, J. (2006). What do teachers teach in introductory programming? Proceedings from ICER '06: *The Second International Workshop on Computing Education Research*. (pp. 17-28). New York, NY: Association for Computing Machinery.

Scratch Web site. (n.d.). Retrieved June 23, 2012, from http://scratch.mit.edu

Siegler, R. (1998). *Children's Thinking*. Upper Saddle River, NJ: Prentice Hall.

Sivilotti, P. A., & Laugel, S. A. (2008). Scratching the surface of advanced topics in software engineering: a workshop module for middle school students. Proceedings from SIGCSE '08: *The 39th SIGCSE Technical Symposium on Computer Science Education*. (pp. 291-295). New York, NY: Association for Computing Machinery.

Soloway, E. M. (1986) Learning to Program = Learning to Construct Mechanisms and Explanations. *Communications of the ACM, 29*, 850-858.

Steffe, L.P., & Gale, J. (1995). *Constructivism in education*. Mahwah, NJ: Lawrence Erlbaum Associates.

Sykes, E. (2007). Determining the effectiveness of the 3D Alice programming environment at the Computer Science I level. *Journal of Educational Computing Research, 36*, 223-244.

Stross, R. (2008). What Has Driven Women Out of Computer Science? *New York Times*, Retrieved from http://www.nytimes.com/2008/11/16/business/16digi.html

Taylor, R. (1980) The computer in the school: tutor, tool, tutee. *Teachers College Press*. 243-245.

Vilner, T., Zur, E., & Tavor, S. (2011). Integrating Greenfoot into CS1: A case study. Proceedings from ITiCSE '11: *The 16th Annual Joint Conference on Innovation and Technology in Computer Science Education*. (pp. 350). New York, NY: Association for Computing Machinery.

West, M., Ross, S. (2002). Retaining females in computer science: A new look at a persistent problem. *Journal of Computing Sciences in Colleges. 17*, 1-7.